Communica

D0784655

One of the most important requirements of leadership is effective communication. The idea that some people are natural leaders and that others will never learn to show good leadership is nowadays outdated. It has been replaced by the conviction that leadership and communication skills can be learnt.

Providing a thorough introduction to skilled interpersonal communication, *Communication in Organizations* consists of three parts. Part I introduces basic communication skills, and makes a distinction between regulating skills, listening skills and sender skills. Part II considers a number of different dialogues: the interview used to gather information, the selection interview, the employment interview, the performance evaluation interview, the personal problems interview, handling complaints, breaking bad news, and the sales interview. Part III is dedicated to conversations in more complex group situations, discussing decision making, conflict management, negotiations, and giving presentations.

Practical examples and concrete conversations are used to give students and professionals straightforward advice on key leadership skills, including motivating people, delegating tasks, leading meetings and overseeing projects. This book will appeal to undergraduate and postgraduate students of psychology as well as those studying business, economics, and the hospitality industry.

Henk T. Van der Molen is professor of psychology at the Institute of Psychology at Erasmus University Rotterdam, The Netherlands and at the Open University of The Netherlands. He is (co-)author of more than 20 books and 100 articles and chapters, many of which concern professional communication skills training. He was President of the Dutch Psychological Society from 1995–2003.

Yvonne H. Gramsbergen-Hoogland studied personality psychology at the University of Groningen. Thereafter she joined the faculty of Economics at the Hanzehogeschool of Groningen, where she was a trainer in interpersonal skills, developing several widely used programmes. She is involved as freelance trainer in human resources management and (co-) author of four books.

Communication in Organizations
Basic Skills and Conversation Models

Henk T. Van der Molen and
Yvonne H. Gramsbergen-Hoogland

Ψ Psychology Press
Taylor & Francis Group
HOVE AND NEW YORK

First published 2005 by Psychology Press
27 Church Road, Hove, East Sussex, BN3 2FA

Simultaneously published in the USA and Canada
by Psychology Press
711 Third Avenue, New York, NY 10017

Psychology Press is part of the Taylor & Francis Group, an informa business

© 2005 Psychology Press
Dutch version © 1995 Yvonne H. Gramsbergen-Hoogland and
Henk T. Van der Molen

Paperback cover design by Anú Design

The publisher makes no representation, express or implied, with
regard to the accuracy of the information contained in this book and
cannot accept any legal responsibility or liability for any errors or
omissions that may be made.

This publication has been produced with paper manufactured to strict
environmental standards and with pulp derived from sustainable
forests.

British Library Cataloguing in Publication Data
A catalogue record for this book is available from the British Library

Library of Congress Cataloging in Publication Data
Molen, Henk T. van der, 1964–
    Communication in organizations : basic skills and conversation
models / Henk T. Van der Molen and Yvonne Gramsbergen-
Hoogland.
        p. cm.
    "Simultaneously published in the USA and Canada."
    Includes bibliographical references and index.
    ISBN 1-84169-555-6 – ISBN 1-84169-556-4 1. Communication in
organizations. 2. Business communication. I. Gramsbergen-Hoogland,
Yvonne H., 1964– II. Title.
    HD30.3.M65 2005
    658.4'5–dc22

                                                2005014960

ISBN 9781-84169-555-6 (hbk)
ISBN 9781-84169-556-3 (pbk)

Typeset in Times by Garfield Morgan, Rhayader, Powys

Printed and bound in Great Britain

Contents

List of tables and figures

Tables

Figures

Preface

Graduates from higher vocational and university education often reach positions in which they have to take the lead. They have to motivate people, delegate tasks, lead meetings and retain an overview. One of the most important requirements is that they are able to communicate effectively. The idea that some people are natural leaders and that others will never learn to give good leadership is nowadays outdated. It has been replaced by the conviction that leadership and communication skills can be learnt. Skilled Interpersonal Communication is part of many curricula in higher education.

This book consists of three parts. In Part I *basic communication skills* are dealt with. A distinction is made between regulating skills, listening skills and sender skills. Part II concerns a number of different *dialogues*: the interview used to gather information, the selection interview, the job application interview, the performance evaluation interview, the personal problems interview, handling complaints, breaking bad news and the sales interview. Part III is dedicated to conversations in more *complex group situations*. The subjects discussed include decision making, leading meetings, conflict management, negotiations and giving presentations. Many practical examples and concrete conversations are used in order to give students a clear perspective on future (leading) positions in an organization.

The book is an adaptation of the Dutch book *Gesprekken in Organisaties* by Yvonne H. Gramsbergen-Hoogland and Henk T. Van der Molen (2003, 3rd ed., Groningen: Wolters-Noordhoff). Yvonne H. Gramsbergen-Hoogland has been a teacher in the Department of Business Economics of the Hanzehogeschool Groningen. Henk T. Van der Molen is professor of psychology at Erasmus University Rotterdam and at the Open University of the Netherlands.

The content of the original book has been adapted to the hospitality industry. The adaptation consisted of changing the original example organization – a building company – into a catering organization and by adding a chapter on handling complaints.

In The Netherlands the book is widely used in the communication skills training programmes of many institutions in higher vocational and university education. After selling 60,000 copies we decided that it might be worthwhile to have it published for the English-speaking market. We hope that this book will prove its importance outside The Netherlands and would be grateful to receive feedback on it.

Henk T. Van der Molen, Rotterdam
Yvonne H. Gramsbergen-Hoogland, Onnen
June 2005

Acknowledgements

This adaptation has been developed with help of Anne Marijke Gerritsen who has been a teacher at the Hotelschool, The Hague.We thank Eveline Osseweijer for the skilful creation of the figures in this book. Furthermore, we express our gratitude to the blind reviewers, whose suggestions have led to substantial improvements of the text. Finally, we thank Penelope Allport for her conscientious editing.

Introduction

Purpose of this book

Organizations are networks of people. These people need to communicate with each other in order to perform the tasks necessary for the realization of the organizational goals. One of the problems that students are faced with when preparing for a managerial task in an organization is the fact that 'organization' and 'communication' are abstract concepts. Concepts like these need to be made concrete. What are the subjects in the communication? Who is involved? What is the purpose of the communication? This book will be useful for students who are being educated for managerial positions. It will help them to develop a theoretical framework for various types of conversations and will give them a guide to learning the skills necessary to hold these conversations in a professional manner. In many respects this is important in order to realize the goals of the organization (Baron & Markman, 2000; Hargie, Dickson, & Tourish, 2004).

Structure of the book

This book consists of three parts. Part I *Basic Communication Skills*, discusses the importance of these skills in almost every professional conversation. These basic skills can be considered the building blocks for the conversation types discussed in Part II, *Dialogues*, and Part III, *Group Conversations*. In Part I a distinction is made between the so-called regulating skills, which are skills used to direct the conversation (Chapter 1), listening skills (Chapter 2) and sender skills (Chapter 3). The basic communication skills are partly based on Ivey's microtraining method (Ivey, 1971; Ivey & Bradford Ivey, 2003) – a step-by-step method in which the complexity of the skills taught increases – and partly from the book *Personal Conversations. Roles and Skills for Counsellors* (Lang, Van der Molen, Trower, & Look, 1990).

Part II contains a number of *dialogues* held by managers in most organizations. The dialogues discussed are: the interview (Chapter 4), the selection interview (Chapter 5), the job application interview (Chapter 6), the performance evaluation interview (Chapter 7), the personal problems interview (Chapter 8), handling complaints (Chapter 9), the bad news interview (Chapter 10) and the sales interview (Chapter 11). In each chapter attention is paid to the structure of the conversation and to the skills necessary to hold the conversation in such a way that its goals will be achieved. This part focuses on the interaction between two conversation partners.

A number of *group conversations* in which more than two people participate are discussed in Part III: decision making (Chapter 12), leading meetings (Chapter 13), conflict management (Chapter 14), negotiating (Chapter 15) and giving presentations (Chapter 16). The main issue in these chapters is the role of the conversation leader, who should be able to handle the complexity caused by the different senders and different receivers in the conversation. He should not only be able to structure the conversation, but also be able to pay attention to the different participants and their contributions and keep sight of the goals of the conversation at the same time.

The practical examples described in the three parts of this book take place at the simulated company Dinner Ltd. We have chosen for this approach since it enables us to describe the application of the skills and conversation models concretely.

How to use this book

Over the last decades we have developed a broad experience in the development and execution of training programmes based on this book (Van der Molen, Hommes, Smit, & Lang, 1995). In these training programmes we focus on three goals:

1   Increasing knowledge and insight about communication skills.
2   Extending the behavioural repertoire of communication skills and conversation models.
3   Increasing self-confidence when dealing with (difficult) professional conversations.

In order to achieve these goals a training methodology based on cognitive social learning principles is used. The following elements can be distinguished:

- theoretical instruction
- modelling
- exercises and role play
- feedback.

Theoretical instruction

Studying this book will give students a cognitive framework. The chapters in Part I contain theoretical background information about every skill separately. Parts II and III contain relevant theoretical information, a conversation model and a description of the skills involved for each specific training subject.

Modelling

After studying the theory, the skill or the conversation model is demonstrated by means of videotape or a role play by the trainer(s). After each demonstration a short discussion on the examples follows, which will help students to increase insight into the effects of effective and ineffective use of communication skills.

Exercises and role play

The students practise the skills and conversation models by means of an exercise or role play. These are observed by fellow students and the trainer. Sometimes the role plays are videotaped. Then the videotape will also be used in the feedback session afterwards.

Feedback

After practising the students receive feedback on the application of the skill(s) or conversation model. One thing we would like to mention here is that reinforcing appropriate behaviour will lead to the highest learning effects (Ivey & Bradford Ivey, 2003). This means that in the debriefing one first discusses the effective actions of the students. Less appropriate actions are discussed in relation to suggestions for improvement.

In Appendix A of this book you will find a number of exercises for each chapter that can be used in training programmes.

Description of Dinner Ltd

Dinner Ltd is a catering organization located in London. Dinner Ltd provides food and beverage for company gatherings and parties. It prepares and serves dinners at locations chosen by the client.

The Managing Director of Dinner Ltd is Freddy Fortune. He studied at the School for Hospitality Service in Manchester. In his last year at this school he founded Dinner Ltd together with Gerald Glass. The company turned out to be very successful. Gerald Glass has a degree in economics and is the Commercial Director. Jenny Jacobson is the Secretary of Dinner Ltd. She is in charge of reception and all secretarial activities.

Middle management consists of the Chef, Bert Berman, the Food and Beverage (F&B) Manager, Harry Haddock, and Charlotte Cohen, who is in charge of the financial department. Bert Berman and Harry Haddock both

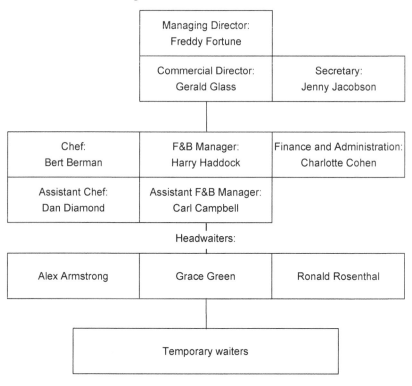

Figure I.1 Organizational structure of Dinner Ltd

have assistants. Dan Diamond is Assistant Chef and Carl Campbell is Assistant F&B Manager.

Three headwaiters, Alex Armstrong, Grace Green and Ronald Rosenthal, are in charge of the waiters – temporary employees who work by the hour. These temporary employees are usually students from various hotel schools in Europe.

Dinner Ltd values good communication. This implies that employees should be aware of the values and norms within the company such as cooperation. Dinner Ltd does not want to appear to be a hierarchical company, which means that orders are seldom given and everybody participates in decision making. The structure of Dinner Ltd is shown in Figure I.1.

Part I

Basic communication skills

Introduction

In every organization where people work together, communication is essential. Discussions are held about the tasks that must be performed, about their relation to one another and about the situations which demand change. There is meeting and organizing to be done. There are appointments to be made. There are contacts to be made with the outside world.

Do you learn this within the framework of the organization? For sure, but you are one step ahead if you have immersed yourself in it in advance and have developed skills that can become sharpened and refined in the practical running of the organization.

For example, when the employees of Dinner Ltd wish to hold the various types of discussions with which they are concerned, and to conduct them in an appropriate manner, a number of building blocks are necessary. We call these building blocks basic communication skills.

In this first part we will discuss the basic communication skills, which are always of interest for communication. In communication a general distinction can be made between the *sender*, the person who sends out a message, and the *receiver*, the person who receives the message (Figure 1.1).

Figure 1.1 Communication between sender and receiver

The same distinction can be made between sender and receiver (or listener) skills. With regard to sender skills we can make a distinction between regulating skills and assertive skills. Regulating skills are those with which one influences the structure and direction of the conversation; these are necessary to monitor the meaningful progress of the conversation. Assertive skills are those whose purpose is to reveal as clearly as possible what one thinks and wants. (For a more extended skill model of interpersonal communication we refer to Hargie & Dickson, 2004, p. 23.)

Part I is structured as follows. In Chapter 1 we discuss the regulating skills. This is followed by the listening skills in Chapter 2. Then in Chapter 3 the assertive skills are dealt with.

With the help of the basic communication skills, all different types of conversations can be held. Whether a selection interview, a job evaluation, a negotiation or a meeting is involved, it is always important that members of staff direct the conversation as well as possible, listen to what others have to say attentively and put across their own opinion and intention as clearly as possible. In other words, acquisition and a thorough command of the skills discussed in these three chapters is necessary to be able to hold the different types of conversation which will be discussed in Part II and Part III.

Before we elaborate further on these skills, we would like to pay some attention to the general understanding of the concept 'skill'. According to *Collins Dictionary* skill means: 'quickness, swiftness; 2) dexterity, proficiency, adroitness'. The concept – as we mean it – is best described by the second definition. At the same time we would like to stress that skills training not only means teaching a few tricks, but also being able to choose as functionally as possible from a 'repertoire of skills'. By 'functionally' we mean that the application of the skills contributes as much as possible to the realization of the goals of the particular conversation.

Practical example

On Monday morning Food and Beverage Manager Harry Haddock is leafing through his diary to see how the week's schedule looks: this afternoon the first of two weekly staff meetings with both directors; tomorrow morning a consultation with the headwaiters about the party next week for a computer company; then two days at a conference in Liverpool about sickness absence. So this week it will be impossible to spend a morning calmly sitting down and preparing a conversation with Alex Armstrong and Charlotte Cohen about the terrible history of the new temporary waiters.

Chef Bert Berman asks where Dan Diamond is hanging out. 'Sick' is the answer. Good heavens, is that man sick on Monday morning again? How should he approach this? That bloke has got to go if it continues like this, which is a shame as he's a good assistant. But you must be able to depend on a bloke. Should he go and talk to him?

Grace Green faces Ronald Rosenthal with it: 'Ronald we must have a talk about the personnel day. When can we talk about it? It's not going so well.'

Freddy Fortune to Gerald Glass: 'Gerald, are you having that meeting with the guy from the kitchen factory this afternoon? Can you come by this morning as I want to have a word about the payment conditions. Maybe we can make them a little more flexible.'

In the secretary's office disaster has struck. Jenny Jacobson says to her colleagues: 'How is it possible that first thing on Monday morning it's such chaos? Are there people sick, are we overworked, or are we just too slow? Mr Fortune wants to see the minutes of the yearly meeting this afternoon. I can't tell him they're not ready yet. We have to talk.'

All these examples make it clear that conversations are essential in a lot of processes, and finally for the success of the organization.

1 Regulating skills

Introduction

The purpose of the regulating skills is to protect the order and clarity of the conversation. Table 1.1 gives an overview of the skills that are discussed in subsequent paragraphs.

Table 1.1 Overview of the regulating skills

- Opening the conversation, setting goals
- Goal evaluation
- Closing the conversation

Opening the conversation, setting goals

When you take the initiative in a conversation, for efficient continuation it is usually important to supply your conversational partner with your intentions fairly soon after beginning. How exactly you open the conversation is naturally dependent upon the situation. When you want to discuss the progress of a project with a colleague who drops in now and then, you would start this conversation differently from when you meet a new client for the first time, or in a selection interview when you meet an applicant. In the first case, you would start fairly informally, whilst in the last case you would usually begin formally. In order to create a relaxed atmosphere, one often begins a conversation by discussing generalities. This can work well, but we must realize that there are many people who do not feel at ease when discussing generalities. These feelings of unease are on the one hand brought about because one has the idea that time is not being efficiently used, and on the other because one does not know exactly how to end the generalities. Such people only begin to feel at ease when you get to the point, namely when the conversation about the important subjects begins.

Whether you start formally or informally, in both cases clarity of your intentions promotes the smooth progression of the conversation. When you have the opportunity to prepare yourself for a conversation, you can try to devise a global structure for it. You should try not to stick to this structure too rigidly in case other turns in the conversation turn out to be more useful, bearing in mind its purpose. In general we can state that a clear conversational structure, upon which the conversational partners have agreed at the beginning, promotes efficiency. In practice, conversational partners will often have a number of subjects they wish to discuss. By making an inventory of these subjects in advance and establishing the order of the subjects to be discussed, you can specify a sort of agenda for the conversation.

Goal evaluation

In this book we assume that conversations are based on a goal. Often the goal is the solving of problems. In order to check that you are still busy with the goals which were originally set, it is useful to ask 'goal evaluating questions' from time to time. These are questions such as: 'What was it exactly we wanted to achieve?' 'Are the goals attainable?' 'Are the methods employed adequate in relation to the goal?' Take an example from the last part of the conversation between Bert Berman and Harry Haddock at the beginning of the week:

HARRY: We were going to discuss the planning for this week. In the meantime we have decided that I will reorder the crates of wine and that you will chase up the butcher. Are there any other things that we need to discuss now?

In this example we see that Haddock refers to the goals set at the beginning of the conversation and then gives Berman a chance to speak. When one or both of them is of the opinion that the planning for the following week has not yet been adequately discussed, they can decide to continue the conversation. If both agree that the goal has been reached, then the conversation can be rounded off. At the end of the conversation it is often useful to summarize the arrangements.

Closing the conversation

In order to keep a check on the time it is generally wiser to make known the time available at the beginning of the conversation. Then a clear agreement has been made about the length of the conversation; for example, half an hour or three-quarters of an hour. If such an agreement is made, it is important to keep an eye on this time too: that is to say, you must decide whether the goals set can be reached within the limited time available. If the time has almost expired, you can refer to the agreement. For example: 'I see that we have about five minutes left.' Then a summary can be introduced with a sentence such as: 'Maybe it is a good idea if we take a look at what we have discussed so far.' After this summary you can discuss with your conversational partner how you will continue. In many cases it is useful to close with a summary, where the concrete arrangements can be lined up (see Chapter 2).

2   Listening skills

Introduction

Not only is it important to have a good structure in a conversation, but it is also important to let your conversational partner know that he is being listened to (Bostrom, 1990; Steil, 1991). First of all it is stimulating for the partner, and second one can avoid the problems that occur when one does not listen well. Burley-Allen (1995) has described listening as 'the forgotten skill', indicating that a lot of people tend to speak too quickly without having paid careful attention to one another. In Table 2.1 we present an overview of the listening skills that are discussed in this chapter.

Table 2.1 Overview of the listening skills

'Non'-selective listening skills; attentive behaviour	Selective listening skills
• Nonverbal behaviour • Minimal encouragers	• Asking questions • Paraphrasing • Reflection of emotions • Concreteness • Summarizing

In the folllowing section on 'non'-selective listening skills it is explained that the listener has only little influence on the conversation. He gives other people all the time to explain their story and only responds by giving attention. These skills are necessary to stimulate the conversation partner into talking. Selective listening skills are used by the listener to find out and select certain aspects of the conversation that he finds important. 'Non'-selective skills are hardly ever used alone. Even when one is only paying attention to somebody's story, one often unconsciously selects what one finds important and gives more attention to that part. That is why we have put 'non' in inverted commas.

'Non'-selective listening skills, minimal encouragers

According to Argyle (1981, 1988) approximately half of our communication is composed of nonverbal behaviour.

Nonverbal behaviour

Facial expression

From your facial expression it can often be seen whether you are interested in what the other person is saying or whether you are elsewhere with your thoughts (Argyle & Cook, 1976). Facial expression is often directly related to your feelings (Russell & Fernandez-Dols, 1997), sometimes even more often than you actually imagine. According to Hackney and Cormier (1979) the most remarkable facial expression is the smile. By smiling you can show interest, kindness, and sympathy, which have stimulating effects on the speaker. However, providing the correct dose of smiling is essential: too much can lead to speakers feeling they are not being taken seriously, or it can show your own insecurity. On the other hand too much frowning can be interpreted as disapproval. Sometimes frowning means that you are trying to understand what the speaker is saying. In that case frowning is an expression of involvement, which stimulates speakers to be more clear and explicit in what they are saying.

Eye contact

The second aspect of nonverbal behaviour is eye contact. Stimulating eye contact means that your eyes should meet the speaker's eyes once in a while. You should neither have a fixed stare, nor should you avoid the speaker's eyes altogether. Staring can make the other person feel uncomfortable. They may get the feeling that they are being studied. Avoiding eye contact often stems from personal insecurity. It is obvious that you are not making a confident impression.

Body posture

A third aspect is body posture. The interest you have in the other person can also be shown by a relaxed and friendly body posture. By assuming a comfortable body position you can make it easy for you to listen. A relaxed conversation partner often evokes more trust than a restless and constantly gesturing one. Making exaggerated gestures is also associated with nervousness (Axtell, 1991). Although not showing any nervousness is not very natural, it is usually more pleasant to talk to someone who emits a certain stability and calmness.

Encouraging gestures

The last aspect of nonverbal behaviour is called encouraging gestures. By nodding and making supportive gestures with the hands and by avoiding nervous and distracting movements, you can show your attention, which will stimulate the speaker to continue talking.

Verbal following

The second 'non'-selective way of showing interest is verbal following. This means that the comments you make should be in line with what the speaker is saying and that you do not start any new subjects. If you follow closely what the speaker is saying, the speaker will be able to finish his train of thought. To understand the speaker fully, it is necessary to put aside your own opinions and thoughts about the subject. In order to do so, you should confine yourself to 'minimal encouragers'.

Minimal encouragers

Minimal encouragers are short verbal reactions intended to stimulate the speaker to talk by showing him that he is being listened to. Examples are: hemming (uh-huh), yes . . . yes, and then?, go on, or even the repetition of one of the words in a questioning tone of voice. These small utterances may not seem of great influence, but their stimulating effect is of importance to the speaker (Greenspoon, 1955).

The skill of 'attentive behaviour, listening' is often considered easy. When the basic attitude is to be attentive and interested in what people are saying, then this 'attentive behaviour' won't cause many problems. However, research has shown that even people who consider themselves good listeners do not listen as well as they think they do. They tend to start questioning too fast or they start reciting their own experiences before the speaker has finished talking. Even more striking were the results that these 'beginners' mistakes' proved to be more the rule than the exception to the rule. As it turned out, it was not only necessary to teach the students appropriate listening behaviour, but also to break certain bad listening habits which had been learnt in everyday life.

Besides the 'non'-selective skills, you will also need to use selective listening skills in most conversations.

Selective listening skills

What is selectivity in a conversation? Selectivity here is related to the fact that in your reactions you give certain aspects of the speaker's conversation more attention than others. You can do that on purpose in order to find out more about the contents of the subject or to get more involved in the feelings expressed. Another way is to give a certain subject in the conversation more attention. We refer here to the example of Dinner Ltd. When one is having a conversation with a client, one can pay attention either to the different choices on the menu for a certain lunch or to the financial aspects. Selectivity determines your immediate reactions to the conversation and the choice of subthemes being discussed. In the second case the concept is broader. The different selective listening skills will be discussed in the following paragraphs.

Asking questions

During many conversations it is often necessary to clarify what speakers are saying exactly and what they really want. We have to deal here with 'problem clarification'. In this phase asking questions will help the speaker to put his thoughts in clear, actual and understandable words. A clear distinction needs to be made between open-ended and closed questions.

Open-ended questions

These questions leave speakers much freedom in formulating answers to them. They can respond in their own words in accordance with their wishes or opinions. An easy way to start these questions is by using words such as 'How?' 'What?' or 'Can you tell me something about?' These questions give the speaker much space to answer freely. Compare the following sentences:

- 'How may I help you?'
- 'What would you like to talk about?'

to:

- 'How is that project doing?'
- 'Can you tell me how you approached that client?'

With the first two questions both the content and form of the reaction are free. The last two questions give less freedom because they are about a selected subject (the project, the approach of the client). But even with this restriction the speaker can answer in any way he wants.

Furthermore we can make a distinction between questions related to the subject that the speaker is talking about and questions not related to the subject. These questions should only be asked when the previous subject has been thoroughly explored.

'Why' questions

The 'why' question is often a suitable open-ended question: in particular because people always have reasons for acting in a certain manner.

Moreover, they have created their own ideas about why they did something and why problems have arisen. However, these types of questions can be regarded as threatening when placed at the beginning of a conversation. When speakers feel they have to justify their actions to the listener right at the beginning, they will feel obliged to give explanations about things they are not ready to answer yet. The chance exists that they will get defensive and confused.

Special attention needs to be paid to the tone of the 'why' question. It can sound like a reprimand – 'Why are you so far behind on the schedule?' – or like an invitation – 'Do you have any idea what the reason is for the delay?' While both questions have the same content, the latter is much more inviting and friendlier in tone and therefore more likely to be answered than the first one.

Closed (directing) questions

These types of question can be answered with a single word, either a yes or a no will usually do. Examples of such questions are:

- 'Do you like that project?'
- 'Have you contacted the bank about the financing yet?'
- 'Do you get along with your colleagues?'
- 'Were you disappointed when you failed the exam?'

You can see that the answers to these questions can be minimized to a simple yes or no. The questions have several negative aspects. First, the speaker is restricted to answer the question. Second, they are often suggestive because these questions stem from preconceived ideas, for example: Chef Berman to headwaiter Green arriving too late for their appointment: 'Did you have a nice party again last night?' From this example we can see that Berman already has an idea of what might be the reason for Green's lateness. The leading question stems from that insinuation. The degree of suggestiveness depends heavily on the tone in which he asks the question. The disadvantageous effect that this kind of question has on the conversation is that the speaker will start to give short and maybe defensive answers. However, it is useful to ask closed questions when you want to find out factual and specific information, or when open-ended questions do not result in much information.

When to ask open-ended or closed questions

When asking questions you have the option of choosing between different kinds. The one you choose depends on the goal you have in mind for the conversation (Dohrenwend, 1965). When you want to give the speaker space to express his views in his own way, you had better ask open-ended questions. When you want to find out something specific in order to see if you understood it correctly, you should ask closed questions. The use of closed questions is also helpful when you want more in-depth information about the subject, for example: 'At what time exactly is the train arriving?' There are no general rules for when to use these type of questions and when not. What is important is that you are able to use any type of question at the correct moment.

Paraphrasing of content

The second selective listening skill is 'paraphrasing of content'. This means *briefly stating in your own words* what the speaker has said. The chief characteristic of paraphrasing is that it is based on *factual information*. This skill serves several functions:

1   Listeners can check that they have understood everything correctly. This is particularly important when the speaker has given a lot of complex and confusing information.
2   The speaker experiences understanding and it might be stimulating to hear their thoughts expressed in other words. Listeners should be very flexible in the way they express themselves.

When applying this skill it is important for listeners not to confuse their own opinions with what the speaker is actually saying. It is therefore important that the paraphrase is expressed in a *questioning* way. This gives the speaker the chance for correction. The use of this skill is important when you have to get a clear picture of, for example, a guest's complaint or when you are given an assignment that you do not completely understand. Here is an example from Dinner Ltd:

GERALD GLASS: From next Tuesday I have to go to Paris for three days. I don't know yet if I'm taking the plane or whether I should go by train. Can you arrange the trip and hotel, Jenny?
JENNY JACOBSON: That's fine, but if I understand it correctly you don't know yet which means of transport you will take. [paraphrase]
GERALD: Well, uh, I prefer to fly, I think . . .
JENNY: OK. So, you will be departing on the coming Tuesday and you will be returning on Thursday. Is that correct? [paraphrase]

Reflection of feelings

The term 'reflection of feelings' literally means mirroring of feelings. According to Hargie and Dickson (2004), reflections 'can be regarded as statements in the interviewer's own words that encapsulate and re-present the essence of the interviewee's previous message' (p. 148; see also Dickson,

1997). The goal of this skill is to show that you are trying to understand how the speaker feels here and now in the conversation.

The first function of reflecting is that speakers notice that their feelings, regardless of their nature, are being understood, accepted and getting attention. Often the intensity of the feelings (e.g. anger) then diminishes. The reflection of them has a soothing effect. The second function of reflection of feelings is a controlling one. You are checking whether you have estimated the feelings of the speaker correctly.

Recognition of feelings and sensitivity to moods is a prerequisite if you want to reflect someone else's feelings correctly. People can show how they feel or how they felt in different ways. They might use 'emotion' words such as 'I am scared', 'I am excited' or 'I feel exhausted'. But usually feelings are shown in nonverbal ways: for example, by the speed of talking, tone of voice, body posture, or by blushing and turning away. All these can be regarded as expressions of how the person is feeling. By being alert to these behavioural manifestations of emotion it can become easier to reflect the other person's feelings.

Feelings can be divided into single or complex feelings. Single feelings can either be positive ('I am happy') or negative ('I am sad'). Complex feelings, in particular, are often confusing and especially arise in emotional situations. Feelings of stress and tension can be both positive and negative. When these kinds of feelings occur it is important that you show consideration for them.

When applying this skill it is important to be on the same wavelength as the speaker. This means that you reflect the other person's feelings with the same intensity as they express them. When someone says 'I feel so listless', then the reaction 'You don't want to live anymore' would be too strong a reflection, and the reaction 'You're a little bored' too weak a reflection. The reflection should be connected to the expression of the feeling(s). This sounds easy, but in practice it is difficult but very important to apply this skill correctly.

The application of this skill is especially important in situations that are highly emotional. An example of a situation in which negative emotions play a part is one in which bad news needs to be conveyed (see Chapter 10). An example in which positive feelings are involved is a situation in which an employee is enthusiastic about a promotion. The next example illustrates how reflection is used in a conversation between Freddy Fortune and secretary Jenny Jacobson:

> Jenny Jacobson is somewhat upset because the typing has been piling up over the last few days and because the managers keep on forgetting to mention where they have gone.

JENNY: I can't go on any more. A client called yesterday and I couldn't tell him where you were or when you would be back in the office again.

FREDDY: I understand this is upsetting you. [reflection of feeling]

JENNY: Yes indeed, and that's not all. Since I have had to handle all those calls, I don't get around to doing all the other work. Look at the stack here that I still have to do!

FREDDY: I can imagine you get irritated [reflection of feeling]. I'll make sure it doesn't happen again. [promise to change]

Concreteness

The meaning of concreteness in conversations is that you let speakers tell their story as concretely and precisely as possible. This is a task that consists of several skills. The skills already mentioned, such as listening, minimal encouragers, asking open and closed questions, paraphrasing and reflecting, all contribute to the concreteness of the conversation. By listening and encouraging you can stimulate speakers to give a detailed expression of the case they want to discuss. When that is not enough, more specific information can be gained by asking open-ended and closed questions. Finally, paraphrasing and detailed descriptions also help to get a clearer picture.

To make sure that the speaker is as concrete as possible, you the listener should make sure your own use of language is as concrete as possible. Many people are inclined to understand stories too fast, based on similar experiences of their own. Doing so can lead to the wrong advice being given. Words such as 'always', 'everything' and 'never' should act as warning bells. In general, undefined statements and generalizations such as the following should be noticed: 'That whole project was a disaster.' Trying to make statements like this concrete usually gives a more finely tuned picture.

How far should you go with concreteness? In general it depends on the goal you have in mind. If, for example, you want to find out why an employee is performing his tasks in a certain manner, you will have to go deeply into the subject and get a very concrete answer. In a first orientating meeting with a client you will have to tolerate more vagueness and lack of clarity.

Summarizing

The goal of summarizing is to give structure to the conversation by ordering the main points. A distinction is made between the summarizing of contents and the summarizing of emotions. With the first the accent lies on the contents (cognitive) aspects of the story, whereas with the second it is more with the aspects of feeling. Usually summaries contain both and the relationship between them is made. The basic difference between summarizing contents and paraphrasing/reflection of feelings is that the summarizing covers a longer time span in the conversation.

Your selectivity and your own ability to select play a larger part in this skill compared to the previous skills described. Because of the large quantity of information that has to be used for this, it is likely that you may forget certain aspects or not express them correctly. That is why it is vital that the summary is made in a questioning tone. Your voice should go up at the end, to indicate this correctly. In a statement your voice goes down at the end. The questioning tone gives speakers the chance to say whether they agree with the summary. To conclude, summarizing has the following functions:

- You can check whether you have understood the speaker correctly.
- You can order the different subthemes and vocalize them.

3 Sender skills

Introduction

In the previous two chapters we have discussed two groups of skills: regulating skills, whose purpose is to guard the useful progress of the conversation, and listening skills, whose purpose is to let the other person know as clearly as possible that you are listening. In many situations you will not only want to listen, but you will also have to say what you think. In this chapter we focus our attention on a number of so-called 'sender skills'. We make a distinction between skills where you take the initiative and skills with which you react to someone. An example of the first is giving information; an example of the second is reacting to criticism. Table 3.1 gives an overview of the different skills that will be elaborated upon in the following sections.

Table 3.1 Overview of the sender skills

Sender skills – initiative	Sender skills – reactive
• Giving information • Making requests and giving instructions • Giving criticism • Situation clarification	• Refusing • Reacting to criticism

Sender skills – initiative

Giving information

As an employee in an organization you often have to give information to other people. During a meeting you may have to present a plan, you may have to explain something to an employee about the progress of a project, you may have to give a client information about a product, or you may have to inform an applicant about a function. The question in this section is how to present information. We discuss four factors, that are of importance to answer this question: structure, simplicity of style, conciseness and attractiveness.

Structure

By structure we mean: the clarity and orderliness of an amount of information. Whenever you are going to give an explanation, it is of importance during preparation to divide it into a number of points. At the beginning of the explanation you can best start with short indications of these points. Then the conversational partners will know what is to follow. After that you discuss the various points, specifying the transitions between them: 'That is what I wanted to say about the first point. Let us now turn to the second.' At the end it is sometimes useful to recapitulate the contents.

Simplicity of style

The conversational partner is most likely to understand the information being presented if you use short sentences, known words and clear wording, and speak in a calm tempo. Someone who wishes to demonstrate their expertise through impressive use of language often achieves the opposite effect in the listener. Notions such as clarity and comprehensibility are, after all, relative. The correct choice of wording is dependent, for example, on the level of education of the conversational partner and the level of his familiarity with the subject. Therefore there are no precise directives to be given. It is very important to be alert to the reaction of the person or persons to whom you speak. Information delivered too simply or too slowly arouses boredom or annoyance, as does complex information given too quickly. The feedback that you receive, either verbally or nonverbally, forms an important source of information for the speaker. When the feedback is negative, for example when the conversational partners begin to yawn or to ask all sorts of questions, then you should try to adjust your use of language. When the feedback is positive, you can naturally continue in the same manner.

Conciseness

Here we wish to emphasize thoroughness, conclusiveness and succinctness. What is essential for the conversation should be set apart, shortly and clearly. Conciseness means, therefore, a certain restriction in the amount of information given.

Attractiveness

It is important to mention a number of methods that you as a speaker can use to hold the attention of the conversational partners and to stimulate them to think and to participate actively. We can classify these methods into two groups: ways to enliven the *content* of the conversation, and ways to strengthen the *relationship* between the speaker and conversational partner(s).

The *content* of the conversation becomes captivating when it is paired with concrete examples and unforced wording in the spoken language. The *relationship* between the speaker and conversational partner(s) is strengthened by the maintenance of contact. If you wish to give clear information, you are forced to concentrate on the task. Sometimes this means that you are so busy with the content that you have no time to keep an eye on the listeners. A possible way to avoid this is to prepare yourself thoroughly for what you wish to say, but this is not always feasible. The second way is to keep noticing the reactions of the listeners during the conversation, and to pause now and then, look around and ask if people can still follow the argument. By using these kinds of questions and by picking up vague, sometimes nonverbal reactions, you make it clear that you are paying attention to the listeners.

Making requests and giving instructions

Every employee in an organization regularly has to ask somebody about something. Sometimes you have to gather information; sometimes you want to get something done. When you are in a leadership position, you often have to give instructions. Although the majority of people do not have many problems with carrying out instructions or setting tasks, everyone does know of situations where they find it difficult. Here are a few examples:

> In Dinner Ltd Jenny Jacobson, who is very conscientious, has difficulty in asking for a day off for a family party. Harry Haddock finds it hard to ask Charlotte Cohen about the progress of last year's financial report. Ronald Rosenthal sometimes finds it difficult to give the temporary waiters the order to get back to work after the lunch break.

Why is it that some people have difficulties in making requests or setting tasks? In general we can name three different reasons for this.

In the first place some people may *lack courage*: they are afraid to stand up for themselves. We saw something like this with Jenny Jacobson.

In the second place such a lack of courage often has a lot to do with the *negative expectations* that one has about the reactions that the request will cause. For example, one is afraid of receiving a negative reaction. The expectations are often based on previous experiences. Harry Haddock knows only too well that last year there was the same problem with regard to the financial report, and that he had a serious argument with Charlotte Cohen. Actually he would rather not recreate such a situation.

The third possible cause is that one does not know how to make the request or give the order. In this case it is a question of *lack of skill*.

Often there is a combination of these three causes. Ronald Rosenthal is not sure how he should get his team back to work. He does not really dare to pull rank because he is afraid that they will see him as authoritarian.

We shall now discuss a number of points that are of importance in making a request or giving of an order. First, you should *consider in advance* exactly which request you wish to make, or which order you want to give. Vague questions give vague answers and vague orders lead to employees not knowing exactly what is expected of them. In the second place you should *choose a good moment* for making a request or giving an order. If Charlotte Cohen is talking with a number of colleagues, then it is not a good moment for Harry Haddock to ask about the progress of the financial report. He would do better to wait until the colleagues have left and Charlotte is alone in her room. It is usually constructive to *make it known that you want to ask something* or say something quickly. Then it is good to *express your request*.

In general three different methods can be classified here: first, the *subassertive* way; second, the *assertive* way; third, the *aggressive* way (Alberti & Emmons, 2001; Hargie & Dickson, 2004). Before giving a concrete example of each way, here is a short explanation of each of these concepts:

- *Subassertive* means: not assertive enough. Other words which mean more or less the same are: timid, shy and self-conscious. When you are subassertive, you let others walk all over you, you are often dependent on others, you don't dare to say what you want and you are afraid of entering into conflict with others (Van der Molen, 1984).
- *Aggressive* means: standing up for yourself, but in an irritating way. You silence others, or you make them ridiculous. Another term which approximates this behaviour is authoritative.
- *Assertive* means: being outspoken, standing up for yourself, being independent, daring to express your feelings. The main principle here is that you are responsible for yourself, that you decide if what you do is 'good' or 'bad'. You do not allow yourself to be influenced by what others think of you, or by what you think that others think of you (Paterson, 2000).

Example of the subassertive style

Jenny Jacobson knocks at the door of Freddy Fortune, who is buried in papers.

JENNY: Sorry to bother you, but could I have a word with you about something?
FREDDY: [looks up disturbed] Yes, you can, but you can see that I'm busy.

JENNY: Well, you see, it's like this . . . my parents will have been married for 55 years in two weeks time and now I would . . . uh . . . if it is not too busy, that is . . . actually I'd like to take that day off . . . I hope you don't mind.

In this example the subassertive style is mainly characterized by the hesitant, submissive tone. Also the use of the word 'actually' often indicates subassertive behaviour. By presenting herself so submissively, she has made it easier for the other party to react negatively to the request. This does not mean that this always happens. The subassertive way does sometimes hold its charms. So Freddy Fortune, who after all has known Jenny for a while, could react quite positively to the request. The question however remains whether or not it is comfortable for people who present themselves subassertively to act in this way. Most of the time they don't like it themselves.

Example of the aggressive style

Harry Haddock has already been waiting two weeks for the draft financial report from Charlotte Cohen. Now it is the middle of March and he has still not seen anything. Charlotte keeps saying how busy she is with it, but according to Harry she spends much too much time gossiping with her colleagues. Now he will just go and ask her how it has progressed. He goes to her room.

HARRY: Say Charlotte, I wanted to talk to you for a minute!
CHARLOTTE: Yes, take a seat.
HARRY: I've come here to ask you again if that financial report is finally getting somewhere. Are you actually busy with it? I get more of the impression that you are trying to make a social report instead of a financial one . . .
CHARLOTTE: Yes Harry, but I . . .
HARRY: Let me finish. I'm sick of it. If the report is not ready by the end of this week, then . . .
CHARLOTTE: [fairly angry by this time] Hey, listen to me for a second. If you speak to me in that tone, then sort it out yourself. Don't think you can speak to me in this way!

The conversation continues like this for a while, but the atmosphere is so acrimonious that both parties part feeling furious, without a concrete decision having been made.

Example of the assertive style

Ronald Rosenthal has been eating with the temporary waiters. The waiters are accustomed to playing a game of cards before their work period actually starts. Then they do not pay much attention to the time.

Whilst Ronald finds it annoying to act as a kind of overseer, it is still part of his job to get them back to work. That is why he seizes the moment at which work should start.

RONALD ROSENTHAL: OK boys, it's 12.30, let's get on with it.
LEO LADLE: [whilst laying a card on the table] Come on Ronald, don't be so precise. We're in the middle of a game.
RONALD ROSENTHAL: All right, finish this round, but after that I would like you to start.
LEO LADLE: OK, that's a deal.

The assertiveness lies primarily in Ronald's calm and resolute tone. At the same time, the assertiveness contains an appeal to the reasonableness of others. In the example we also see that Leo Ladle wants to put Ronald's patience to the test, but because he remains calm and reasonable ('All right finish this round, but after that I would like you to start'), his request is then initiated. The phrase 'I would like you to . . .' is also important to the wording. By saying this Ronald makes clear what he wants, without doing so in an authoritative way.

Within this context it is relevant to point out that in western culture over the past decades a change has taken place whereby the authority derived from titles, expertise and hierarchical relations is not automatically accepted in many sectors of society. The authority establishment has developed into a negotiation establishment. This means that nowadays leaders can make their wishes known to employees in the form of orders far less than they could previously.

Giving criticism

Giving criticism is often experienced as difficult. There are several reasons for this. In the first place you may be afraid that the relationship with the person you are criticizing will be altered. They may react indignantly or aggressively, for example. Sometimes one's own insecurity or fear of not being taken seriously enough may play a part. All this can lead to a decision not to give any criticism. Such a decision is often unsatisfactory in the long term, especially when the reasons for criticism continue to exist.

We now make a distinction between criticism of *opinion* and criticism of *behaviour*: that is to say, it can be criticism of the opinion or behaviour of one person, of a group of people or even of an organization. Here we shall limit ourselves to giving criticism to people.

Giving criticism of an opinion

The giving of criticism of an opinion aims to change the other party's mind. How can you best make such criticism? In general it is important that your own behaviour is clear. This means that you express your criticism *openly* and *fairly*. It is not only the tone of voice in which you say something that indicates you disagree with the other person, but also that you state it clearly: 'I disagree with that view, because . . .' If the criticism is only implicitly apparent from your tone, it can often be taken as an accusation, with the risk that the conversation ends in argument.

In order to *dare* to express criticism, you must *feel* self-confident enough. We have already said that many people are afraid of the other's reaction when giving criticism. General points to take into consideration when giving criticism of an opinion are as follows:

- Make sure that you indicate clearly which aspects you are criticizing.
- Speak in 'I terms': 'I find', 'I think' – 'You are', 'You think'. By speaking in 'I terms' you keep the criticism to yourself and you are less accusing.
- Find out if the other really understands what you mean.
- Give the other a chance to reply: for example, by asking 'What do you think about it?'
- If possible try to find a solution together.

Giving criticism of someone's behaviour

An important mistake that is often made when criticizing someone's behaviour is to generalize: for example, when someone has done something wrong, we may have a tendency to think and/or say that they will always do it wrong. This tendency can find expression in our criticism: for example, 'You are always late.' It is really better to keep criticism to specific behaviour rather than to make generalizations. Comparable to criticizing someone's opinion, it is important when criticizing someone's behaviour that your own behaviour is open and clear: for example, 'I find it annoying that you came in late twice this week.' By limiting yourself to concrete behaviour, you make it easier for the other to react.

This also means that you must feel confident enough to dare to give the criticism. You can be afraid that the other will become angry. If you are really convinced that your criticism is justified, then this fear is ungrounded. Second, if the other person does become angry, annoying as this might be, this anger is entirely his own responsibility. Above all, you know how you can react to this anger (see pp. 17–18). An example follows:

> Bert Berman has plucked up the courage and one day he asks his assistant Dan Diamond if he can come to his office at the end of the afternoon. At the arranged time Diamond steps in.

BERT: Take a seat, Danny. I just want to speak with you about something. Frankly, I find it troublesome that for the last three weeks you have called in sick on Monday mornings. What is actually wrong at that time?

Situation clarification

By situation clarification we mean: the skill of perceiving emerging problems or misunderstandings in time, realizing their importance and discussing them. This skill is important in many situations, namely at moments when mutual expectations are no longer in tune with each other. The goal of the skill is to bring about or restore the clarity of the conversation. This skill is somewhat more complex than those previously discussed. When applying it, there is a *conversation about the conversation*. This is also called *meta-communication* or *meta-conversation*. With meta-communication you take some distance from the conversation that you are holding at that moment (Kouwer, 1973). Figure 3.1 shows the two conversation levels.

To clarify further we give a few concrete situations where the application of this skill is useful. First, a situation where someone is addressed about responsibilities that he does not have:

Grace Green and Ronald Rosenthal are having a conversation about the staff's day out.

GRACE: So we agree that we need to hold a survey amongst all staff members. Depending on the outcome, we must then make sure we get a better programme for the day. After all we must ensure that the atmosphere at work improves.
RONALD: Wait a second, let me just clear up a few things. I will be glad to help think about the staff's day out, and also to join in helping with the organization, but I most decidedly do not feel responsible for the atmosphere. We need to create the conditions where it is possible for others to make the atmosphere, I think.

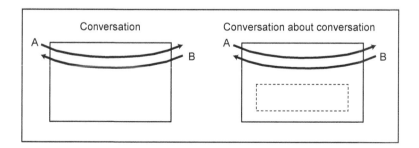

Figure 3.1 Meta-communication

Now we discuss a situation where the conversational partner jumps from one subject to another. It is then useful to signal this, and to agree to pay more attention to each subject:

Harry Haddock drops in on Bert Berman.

HARRY: I've just come to see how the menu for Compudate is going. Carl and I would like to make an appointment with the head of their staff club. By the way, did you ever hear anything about the problem that Charlotte had with the estimate for Simon? Was it miscalculated or not?

BERT: To start with that last point: no, it was not miscalculated, but . . .

HARRY: Talking about calculations, I must tell you such a strange story that I heard at Quack's. They started a new project and now . . .

BERT: Sorry Harry, can I just interrupt. I've got the impression that we are discussing different things at the same time. I suggest we work through them one by one. What do you think?

Sender skills – reactive

Refusing

In organizations it is not only common to ask other people something, but frequently you also receive requests. If you wish to fulfil the request there is usually no problem. It becomes more difficult when you do not find the request reasonable, or you do not have the time. In general, there are three possible ways of reacting.

- *Subassertive*: even though you do not see the reasonableness of the request, you fulfil it. If you do what the other person wants, the result is that this person is content. However, most of the times you are left with a feeling of dissatisfaction, because you did something that you did not actually want to do.
- *Aggressive*: you indicate in an unfriendly tone what you think of the request and you refuse to do it. Often the result is that the other feels insulted and the atmosphere is detrimentally influenced.
- *Assertive*: in a friendly but resolute way you say that you do not wish to fulfil the request and why. In this way you stand up for yourself and you are clear to the other person. If the other insists, you repeat calmly that you don't want to do it.

When refusing or saying no, you can make use of the following points:

1 Listen carefully to the other person's request.
2 Ask for further explanation if you still do not understand something.

3   Say no, calmly and clearly.
4   Explain why you say no.

Here is an example:

> Jenny Jacobson is critical of the manner in which Gerald Glass dele-
> gates tasks and she refuses to carry them out.

GERALD: I am a bit late with this text for the report, but it has to be ready
   to go this week or I will end up with problems. You will manage to do
   it, won't you Jenny?
JENNY: Gerald, I am so terribly fed up with this. Always too late with the
   reports, never an announcement in advance that work is coming up . . .
   And then your cajoling way. Jenny will manage to do it. No, Jenny will
   not manage to do it anymore. Not now, not ever. [She flings the report
   on the table]

According to us, Jenny could have remained on a better footing with
Gerald for longer if she had started by avoiding those little words 'always'
and 'never' and had not blamed him. She could have rejected him like this:

JENNY: Gerald, you are asking me if I can type out the whole report this
   week, in between doing everything else. Why would you get into
   trouble if it were not ready this week?
GERALD: I'm already so late with it, and I find that annoying.
JENNY: Well, I'm sorry, but I can't do it this week. I need to plan my
   activities really well for the whole week. This week is already completely full with tasks equally important as yours.
GERALD: Jenny, I have already promised that they will get the report at the
   end of this week.
JENNY: It's annoying for you, I understand that, but this week I cannot
   manage it. I will start on it first thing next week. Then perhaps it will be
   ready two days later.

Reacting to criticism

We have already discussed how to give criticism. It is of course also possible
that you will receive criticism, whether about your opinion or your behaviour. How should you best react?

Reacting to criticism of your opinion

In general it is important to listen calmly to what the other says, and not to
start apologizing immediately. Then there are various possibilities. In the
first place, you can agree with the other person's criticism. In this case you

can revise your opinion and agree with them. In the second place it is possible that you do *not* agree with the criticism. In that case you begin with a *paraphrase* of what the other person has said: 'I understand that you think like this about it, but my opinion is that . . ., because . . .'. You may convince the other person, but people can also remain true to their opinions. In situations such as this it is a question of *difference of opinion*. Often it is better to establish that there is indeed a difference of opinion rather than endlessly bickering about who is right. In fact, you are then holding a *meta-conversation*. Sometimes the conclusion may be that you want to hear the opinion of a third party in order to reach a definite point of view or conclusion.

Reacting to criticism about your behaviour

Whenever you receive criticism about your behaviour, you can follow roughly the same scenario. This entails first listening calmly, and seeing if you understand the other person's criticism. If you do not understand the criticism, you can ask them to clarify it. If you listen calmly, then you can also better decide whether the criticism is meant accusingly or constructively. If the criticism is accusing, then you can react to it: 'I get the impression that you are blaming me for . . .' If you take the criticism as constructive, the reaction will take this into account. In both cases you will have to delve into it further: which part of the criticism do you agree with, which part you don't agree with. If you agree with it, you can say: 'I know what you mean. Let me try to explain how it came about.' After the explanation you can also indicate that you will try to behave differently in future. When you do not agree with the criticism, you can react with: 'I know what you mean, but I do not agree with it because . . .' In summary, the following points are of importance when reacting to criticism.

1   Listen carefully and try to remain as calm as possible.
2   Ask for clarification or explanation if you still do not understand something.
3   State what you agree with.
4   State what you don't agree with.
5   Explain how it came about.
6   Say what you are going to do about it.

Part II

Dialogues

Introduction

In Part I we discussed a series of basic communication skills. In Part II we deal with several different types of dialogue. For each of the dialogues a conversational model will be presented. A common feature of these models is that there is a structure to the phases involved in the conversations. For each phase an explanation is also given of its most important goals. We also look at which basic communication skills should be used in order to reach those goals.

Which different conversations are actually involved? Chapter 4 deals with *interviews*. The interview is a method of making a systematic analysis of opinions about a certain subject.

Before one gets to be an employee of a company, one usually has to go through a selection procedure. Chapter 5 therefore deals with the *selection interview* and is written from the point of view of the selector or selection committee. In this chapter a model is presented of how to gather information in a systematic and honest way about the suitability of different applicants for the jobs they are applying for.

Chapter 6 deals with *job application interviews*, and treats the subject of conversations from a different angle than the other chapters in Part II. Those chapters deal with conversations where the people involved are already working in a company. Chapter 6 is from the point of view of a person not yet working for the company, but actually trying to get a job there. As this book is meant to serve as an aid for students studying different subjects who are still faced with acquiring a position in the marketplace, it seemed useful to include a chapter which deals specifically with the communication skills necessary for job applicants.

Once one is actually working in a company, one's job role usually serves a specific function. In Chapter 7 *the performance evaluation interview* is discussed. The purpose of this type of conversation is to balance out the interests of the individual employee against those of the company in an optimal way. In this case not only is the functioning of the employee a subject for discussion, but also that of the managerial position. This conversation type is contrasted with the job evaluation interview, which is more of a one-way conversation, where a manager assesses the prospective employee. The performance evaluation interview often includes decisions regarding promotions and salary increases. In this chapter we limit ourselves to a model for the performance evaluation interview. No separate model for the appraisal interview is presented because there is not much of a dialogue going on. It is more a one-way assessment that should be delivered as clearly as possible.

When dealing with employees as a manager you often get confronted with their personal problems. Sometimes employees may talk about themselves, but occasionally it may be necessary to take the initiative to discuss problems, especially if you suspect that they are influencing the way an employee is performing. In Chapter 8 a model is presented for the *conversation on personal problems*.

A manager in the hospitality industry is often confronted with guests' complaints. *Handling complaints* can be a delicate affair. Chapter 9 describes a model which aims to ensure a good relationship with guests or clients.

When a company is manufacturing a product it is also necessary for them to sell it. Chapter 10 deals with a model on *sales interviews*.

From time to time people in organizational management positions need to deliver bad news: for example, when an employee does not get a promotion, or when a reorganization has to be announced. Chapter 11 describes the three-phase model for a *bad news interview*. The most common mistakes made in this type of conversation are also discussed.

Each chapter is structured as follows: it starts with an example from Dinner Ltd; then the *theory* of the conversational model is discussed; this theory is translated into practice; each chapter ends with a summarizing overview.

4 Interviewing

Practical example

Once a fortnight a management meeting takes place at Dinner Ltd. The following people are present: Managing Director, Freddy Fortune; Commercial Director, Gerald Glass; Chef, Bert Berman; Assistant Chef, Dan Diamond; F&B Manager, Harry Haddock; Assistant F&B Manager, Carl Campbell; Head of Finance and Administration, Charlotte Cohen; Secretary, Jenny Jacobson. At the last session it had been decided that the possibilities for partial automation of the menu prices and menu planning would be investigated. It would be possible to automate the planning of menus that did not differ too much.

Both positive and negative aspects were involved in this implementation. The first positive aspect is that the application of standard programs often used in hotel chains would enable them to work faster and thus more efficiently. The computer could replace the manual planning of a standard menu. A second positive aspect is that by implementing computer standard planning, more time will be available for the specific custom-made menus, such as menu planning for theme parties. Negative aspects are that implementation costs are high and employees would have to be retrained. The retraining would probably be met with opposition. Harry Haddock expects that his headwaiters will not be thrilled to exchange pen and paper for a computer. He proposes to the meeting that conversations should be held with all the employees in his department in order to find out what their thoughts are about automation in general and what they see as possible tasks that could be eliminated. His proposition is accepted. Harry goes ahead with preparations for the interviews.

Introduction

The interview can be used to find out people's opinions. Systematic handling of the interview procedure has as its goal to obtain information on a previously determined subject. Three types of interview can be distinguished:

the open interview, the semi-structured interview, the standardized interview (see Keats, 2000).

The open interview

With the open interview only the theme of the conversation is decided in advance. After the interviewer has posed an open question with regard to the theme, interviewees can freely follow their own train of thought and say what they consider important. The interviewer guides the conversation by going more deeply into relevant aspects of the subject.

One disadvantage of this method of interviewing is that the final data are often difficult to process. Each respondent has given an individual answer. These answers can be categorized but it takes a lot of time and effort. In the first place it is often difficult to come up with the categories into which the answers can be put. Second, each answer requires a separate decision on which of the categories it belongs to. This often leads to unreliability of data. Moreover, the interviewer is often faced with a large 'others category', where answers cannot be classified under a set category.

Regardless of all these objections, there are situations where an open interview is the best way to obtain answers. This is true for all situations where it is important that interviewees should be able to allow their thoughts to flow freely, which can lead to the discovery of new aspects of a problem that might otherwise not have been discussed.

The semi-structured interview

With the semi-structured interview the theme about which information needs to be gained is split up into several subthemes. Interviewees are not free to choose the subjects to be discussed, although they are free to answer them in their own way. The interviewer does not have to follow a strict order of subjects. The goal is to deal with all the subjects within the conversation. The interviewer usually starts each new subject with an open question and tries to use basic listening skills in order to get as much information on the subject as possible (see pp. 13–20).

The standardized interview

The standardized interview consists of a questionnaire or some other survey where both the answering categories and the order of answering are pre-determined. The interviewee has to choose answers provided by the interviewer. This procedure has as an advantage that the data can be processed fast and easily (Fowler & Mangione, 1990). However, it offers little opportunity for original ideas or opinions.

Depending on the situation, a choice has to be made between these three interview types within a company. The choice will be the open interview when interviewers are seeking to form an opinion about the functioning of the internal communication system. They can use it to find out where information is stagnating and get ideas for improvements. If the goal of the interviewer is to hear the opinion of colleagues about a certain subject where certain questions need to be answered, then the semi-structured interview is preferable.

If a company wants to conduct an investigation into consumer behaviour or market research in general, they will usually choose a standardized interview. The organization is interested in very specific answers to very specific questions, where the answers can easily be processed. It is important in such interviews to get as many responses as possible in a relatively short time period.

In this chapter we limit ourselves to discussion of the semi-structured interview. When using standardized interviews or surveys one only has to read the interviewee the questions and note down the answers. When discussing the conversational technique of this type of interview, not much more can be added to it than that the interviewer has to pose the questions, which are already on paper, in a neutral tone of voice, therefore not suggestively. Much of what is said about the semi-structured interview is also applicable to the open interview. First we discuss the *preparation* of this type of interview and then the *execution* of the interview. We explain the various steps with the aid of an example from Dinner Ltd and end with a summary.

Preparation of the semi-structured interview

Construction of the interview scheme

The preparation of the semi-structured interview begins with setting up an interviewing scheme. We do this by dividing the main theme into several subthemes. Then for each subtheme several questions are formulated. In the previously discussed example, the main theme is the opinions of the employees about the automation of menu prices and menu planning. Subthemes of automation could be: (dis)satisfaction with the current situation, problems with work processes, possibilities for improvements, or the expected results of automation.

Within each subtheme both open-ended and closed questions can be predetermined. Closed questions ask for specific information, such as how much time certain parts of a task take to be completed. Open-ended questions are used when appreciation of certain parts of the task or situation is involved. The interview scheme forms the skeleton of the interview (see Figure 4.1).

Within the subtheme *current situation* the following questions could be asked:

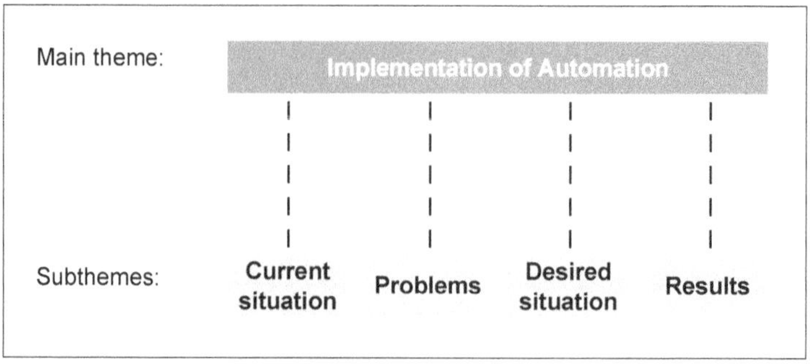

Main theme:	Implementation of Automation			
	│ │ │ │ │ │ │ │			
Subthemes:	Current situation	Problems	Desired situation	Results

Figure 4.1 Interview scheme regarding automation

- Can you give a description of your daily tasks?
- How many aspects does that task consist of?
- How do you feel about the time division?
- What do you like about it?
- What do you like less/dislike about it?
- Which part would you like to spend more/less time on?

In this manner questions can be formulated for each subtheme. In addition to the different questions, each subtheme should include a question for the interviewee about any extra comments/additions: for example, 'Would you like to say something about the situation as it currently exists?'

Clarity beforehand

After the interview scheme has been composed, appointments are made for the interviews. When making the appointments it is important to be clear about the duration and purpose of the interview beforehand. If you don't do that, you run the risk that the employees to be interviewed may draw the wrong conclusions about the reasons for the interviews. The open and honest attitude of the interviewer will increase the willingness to cooperate.

Holding semi-structured interviews

The holding of the interview consists of three phases: *introducing* the interview, following the *interview scheme*, *closing* the interview. We elaborate on each phase below.

Introducing the interview

When starting the interview it is important to include a short period, a so-called 'warming up'. In this situation the interviewer and interviewee can get used to each other through the exchange of some general information, some chit-chat. The interviewer needs to pay attention to what the interviewee says. Then the introduction to the interview follows naturally. The interviewer states clearly once again the duration and purpose of the interview. It is also important to state the order of the interview as you follow the interview scheme: the procedure of the interview. The interviewee now knows what he can expect and is able to cooperate in keeping to the order of the scheme (see p. 9). The interviewer finally makes it clear how the information gained will be used and ensures, if necessary, confidentiality. It speaks for itself that a head of department who has breached the confidentiality of his employees should not expect to receive confidential information in the future.

Following the interview scheme

The middle section of the interview skeleton consists of following the interview scheme. This part takes up the majority of the time and the interviewer makes use of the basic communication skills discussed in Part I.

By showing attentive behaviour, the interviewer creates a quiet and relaxed atmosphere. With the aid of open-ended and closed questions the interviewer gains specific information about the facts and ideas, opinions and views of the interviewee. By making the information concrete, the ideas, opinions and views are made more specific.

By paraphrasing and using reflection of feelings the interviewer displays paying close attention with the consequence that the interviewee feels understood. These last two skills can also be used by interviewers to check whether they really do have a good understanding. If this is not the case, the latter can correct the mistake. By making use of summaries, interviewers can close a subtheme, after which they need to make an explicit transition to the next subtheme.

Closing the interview

When all questions from the interview scheme have been asked, the conversation is ready to be closed. The interviewer needs to indicate that the end of the interview is coming soon. Before interviewers actually end the conversation, they can give the interviewee the opportunity to address subjects they consider relevant. Maybe there are still some questions that the interviewee would like the interviewer to answer which the interviewer had not been able to go into previously. Furthermore interviewees should be informed about the approximate time it will take to process the results of the interviews, and also whether and when they will be able to see a report about them. Finally, a word of thanks is appropriate for the time and effort the employee has given to taking part. (Figure 4.2 presents and overview of the semi-structured interview.)

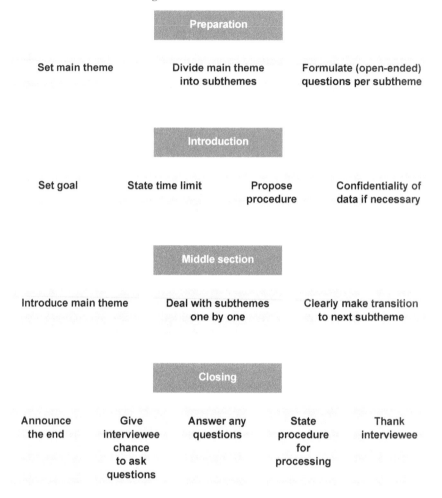

Figure 4.2 Overview of a semi-structured interview

5 The selection interview

Practical example

Carl Campbell, Assistant F&B Manager is going to retire within a short period. Freddy Fortune and F&B Manager Harry Haddock believe that the vacancy will need to be filled as soon as possible. In the twice-weekly management meeting it is decided that a closed selection procedure will be initiated. First a selection committee is to be set up, consisting of Freddy Fortune, Harry Haddock and Grace Green. It is decided that Harry Haddock will make a start by doing a function analysis. When this analysis has been discussed with Carl Campbell among others, an advertisement can be drawn up.

The text of such an advertisement is not easy to write. In order to ensure that the text is as informative as possible, Harry Haddock divides it into five information blocks:

1 An overview of Dinner Ltd and the F&B department
2 An overview of the vacant position
3 An overview of the task demands, prerequisites and wishes of the organization
4 An overview of the labour conditions
5 Extra information.

When the text has been discussed by the committee members, the advertisement will be placed in several large daily newspapers. Applicants interested in the job need to respond within 14 days.

About 20 people reply to the advertisement. The first task of the selection committee is to select application letters according to certain criteria:

• number of years of experience in a similar function
• extent to which the applicant satisfies the formulated function demands.

Each member of the committee reads and judges the letters individually. In a decision-making meeting the applicants are compared. Finally five applicants are invited to an interview and the other fifteen are informed in writing that they have not been selected. One of the five applicants is Ken Klein. He is expected at Dinner Ltd on Wednesday at 10 o'clock. The Chairman of the selection committee is Harry Haddock. Together with Freddy Fortune and Grace Green it has been decided who will pose which questions. Each interview is scheduled to last 45 minutes.

Introduction

As we saw in the practical example, the selection interview is *part of the selection procedure*. Important steps include making a function analysis, setting up the advertisement, providing information about the organization and the task to be performed to interested parties, and making an application letter selection. These parts will not be dealt with in detail in this book. We concentrate here on the *selection interview*.

Furthermore it should be noted that in many companies the selection of personnel is deferred to professional recruitment and selection agencies. In such a case the entire procedure is performed by the agency, after which a few applicants are proposed for the job. However, in most cases the representatives of the company involved will want to hold their own interviews with the proposed applicants.

In the next section we discuss the most important goals of the selection interview. We then discuss a method to use to reach those goals. We focus on the attitude that one has to adopt when holding a selection interview and the skills that fit the different phases of the conversation. Finally, we give a summary of the conversation model.

Goals

The primary goal of the interview is to develop a relationship between the applicant and the interviewer(s) so that the applicant feels comfortable enough to be open and sincere during the conversation. A selection interview may be perceived as somewhat threatening to an applicant who does not know what to expect, perhaps trying to hide one's weaknesses and putting up a smokescreen. In order to avoid this as much as possible it is very important to try to make the applicant feel at ease.

The second goal of the interview is to obtain as much relevant information as possible from the applicant. It should be predictable on the basis of that information whether the applicant is suitable for the job. In practice the selection interview is not only a predictive tool, but also a way to get a personal impression of the applicant. One needs to realize in this case that the subjective impression that one obtains during an interview is not very reliable as a predictive factor.

Method

The selector or selection committee needs to obtain information from the applicant within a limited period of time. In order to be able to *compare* the applicants correctly, each interview should be conducted with the *same methodical structure*.

Good preparation is essential to ensure an efficient, structured interview. Therefore it is wise to make an interview scheme or checklist in advance, noting the themes that you want to discuss. Often the conversation is set up as follows:

1   *Motives for application for the job*
- Why is this position attractive to the applicant?
- What is the reason for the application?
2   *Working through the resumé*
(a) Education
- Why did the applicant choose a certain education?
- What were the achievements of the applicant in that education?
- Which subjects/majors did the applicant choose?
- What further ambitions, e.g. further studies, does the applicant have?
(b) Working experience including present employment
- What positions has the applicant held before the current one?
- What did the applicant like in those functions?
- What are the current tasks?
- Which tasks go well according to the applicant?
- Which tasks do not go well?
(c) Unclear issues
- Where are the 'holes' in the resumé?
3   *Content of the position and task demands*
- Which of the requirements does the applicant fulfil?
- Which are the weak and strong points?
- What are these based on?
- Can the applicant give examples of similar situations which he has experienced in the past?

In addition to this last point, in personnel psychology it is a well-known law that someone's behaviour in the past is the best predictor for someone's behaviour in the future. That is to say one needs to get information about the *behaviour* of the applicant in situations that are comparable with the ones he will find in the new working environment. In order to obtain this information the selector can make use of the so-called STAR model. The STAR model is constructed according to the following four questions:

S: What was the *situation*?
T: Which *task* did the applicant have in this situation?

A: What was the *action* of the applicant? What did he/she then do?
R: What was the *result* of this action?

The different themes mentioned above cannot always be taken separately. As the conversation moves along one can skip parts that have already been covered before.

Basic attitude

In a selection interview the interests of the company are the central points. That does not mean that the interests of the applicants are not involved. It is also of great importance that the latter ends up in a position where justice is done to both their capacities and interests. The fact that the selection committee acts in the interests of the company or organization means that the company's interests determine the structure and themes of the interview. Within the interview structure and themes the committee has to allow applicants to present themselves as well as possible. This entails making them feel at ease at the beginning of the interview and taking a relaxed and inviting attitude. However, one also has to obtain the required information within a limited period of time. This means working in a businesslike and goal-oriented way with the applicant, including even having to be strict in getting precise answers when they are not clearly answered. Depending on the phase of the interview and the applicant's way of answering, the emphasis will either be on using an inviting tone or on using a persistent way of questioning.

Skills in the different phases of the interview

Now we discuss the different phases of the interview, together with the most important skills for the selection committee. Successively we discuss: the start of the interview, providing information about the organization and the vacancy, the interview itself and enabling the applicant to ask questions, summary of the follow-up procedure, and closing of the interview.

The start of the interview

Usually the applicant will be waiting in the foyer or waiting room. The chairman of the committee will get the applicant and introduce himself. Next they proceed to the place where the interview will take place. The applicant is introduced to the other members of the selection committee and invited to be seated.

When applicants look very nervous, the chairman can make them feel at ease by making a few remarks: for example: 'Were you able to find the building easily?' Perhaps a cup of coffee or tea may be offered, after which the actual interview begins. The chairman gives information on the amount of time for the interview and its specific goal:

> In the first place this interview is meant for us to provide you with some information about our organization and about the department for which we are looking for a new employee. You can then form an image of our company and may be able to judge if you might feel at home within it. This conversation is secondly meant for us to get information from you about your capacities for this function. We will mainly look for experiences in your present and previous jobs, and will ask most questions about this subject.

At the same time he describes the global structure of the conversation:

> First we want to provide you with information about our company and about the vacancy. After that we want to ask you some questions. At the end of the interview you will be given the opportunity to ask us questions, and finally we will inform you about the rest of the selection procedure.

Skill

Giving information about the goal and structure of the interview in a clear and concise way.

Information about the organization and the position

In order to provide the applicant with a clear picture about the tasks, the chairman of the selection committee starts off by providing some background information about the company. Subjects discussed include:

- What are the most important goals of the company?
- How is the organization set up? (perhaps presenting a diagram of the organizational structure)?
- What activities are carried out by the organization?
- What were the most important projects of the last few years?

After this overview the chairman moves on to the vacant position and discusses the following themes:

- What are the most important tasks and responsibilities?
- To whom is the employee accountable?

In some cases this phase can be kept very short: for example, when the applicant has received information about the organization and position at a prior stage.

Skills

Giving information about the company and the vacant position: structure, conciseness, and attractiveness of this information are important (see pp. 21–23). The committee members should realize that there is a two-way interaction: they have to decide whether the applicant is suitable for the function, while the applicant has to decide whether the goals and people in this organization are attractive enough for them to want to work there.

The interview

Before the committee members start asking questions, the applicant gets the opportunity to clarify the application. Usually one already has information, in particular the application letter. The chairman can mention that letter by asking an open question:

> You have applied for the position of . . . The reasons for your application you have already mentioned in your application letter, but I would like you to explain in more detail the reasons why you are interested in this job.

After the applicant has given more detailed information, one follows up with a few closing and connecting questions and moves on to the various themes of the interview scheme (see p. 43). When the committee has received sufficient information on a certain theme, it moves on to the next one. For example, a committee member can round off a theme by saying: 'I believe I have got a clear picture of your academic achievement.' The next theme can then begin with an open question: 'Now we would like to know more about your current job. Could you tell us something about that?'

After the applicant has given an answer the interviewer keeps on asking until a complete and concise overview has been obtained. During the interview the checklist should be regularly checked. It is very common to adhere to a structured scheme. When a member of the committee is going to discuss a theme whose relevance is not very clear, it should be explained to the applicant why the question is necessary.

Skills

1   *Attentive behaviour*, to stimulate the applicant to tell more.
2   *Minimal encouragers*, to stimulate the applicant to keep on talking.

3 *Asking questions*. These questions should be clear, not suggestive and preferably open ended: for example, 'What do you like about this position?' The use of closed questions is only recommended for obtaining specific information, for example, 'Do you have a driving licence?' or 'Are you willing to move?'.

4 *Paraphrasing*, when the given information is unclear: for example, 'If I understand you correctly, you did not take decisions independently in your prior job.'

5 *Reflection of feelings*. You can show understanding about what the applicant is saying in a limited way, but you should not go deeply into those feelings: for example, 'I see that it gave you a sense of accomplishment.'

6 *Regulating skills*, such as maintaining the structure of the interview and moving on to a new theme, sometimes also the repeating of the goal of the interview: for example: 'I would now like to know a bit more about your experiences in your former positions' [new theme]. 'Could you start by explaining what your responsibilities are in your current position?' [aspect of interest within the theme]. 'Could you explain in even more detail how many people you have been responsible for?' [applicant seems slightly irritated]. 'Yes, as you notice, I am quite thorough in certain areas, but that is necessary to get a clear picture of your work experience.'

7 *Summarizing* what has been said by the applicant: for example, 'So, you find it especially interesting to work independently, and that is what seems attractive to you in this vacant position?'

8 *Concreteness*, if the information is not clear (we refer here to strictness and perseverance in attitude): for example, 'What exactly do you mean by "making sure that all runs smoothly"? What exactly happens?' 'I still don't exactly understand it. You say "together with the supervisor", but who is doing what exactly?'

9 *Criticizing* may also be necessary when there are contradictory issues in the applicant's story: for example, 'You just said that you prefer to work alone, and now you are saying that you find working as part of a team very interesting. Can you explain this?' One can also criticize by relating it to an observation: for example, 'You say that you would like to work in a more representative position, but you dress quite casually, if I may remark; not in a way that we call representative in our company.'

10 *Situation clarification*, when one notices that the applicant is getting a bit irritated because of the insistent questioning: for example, 'I'm getting the impression that you are viewing my questions as a sort of attack. I don't mean to do this. However, when I have to judge whether you are suitable for this function, I need this kind of information. Do you understand that?'

Giving the opportunity to ask questions, overview of the procedure and closing of interview

When the committee has obtained enough information, the applicant then gets the chance to ask questions in return. Once these have been answered, the remaining selection procedure is briefly discussed and outlined as clearly as possible. Therefore the response should not be: 'You will hear from us as soon as possible.' An example would be: 'This week the selection committee will make a first selection. You can expect a reply from us during next week to indicate whether you will be participating in the next round. This second round of interviews will take place in the period . . . .' Additionally: 'Where can you be reached by phone?'

Applicants also have to be asked whether they themselves are willing to proceed after this interview. Sometimes a psychological assessment is part of the procedure. If so, that should be explained to the applicant. It should also be explained where and when any travelling expenses can be declared and refunded: 'You can claim your travel expenses from the secretary. I will walk with you to the administrative office.' Finally, the applicant is led to the door and thanked for coming. (See Figure 5.1 for an overview of the selection interview.)

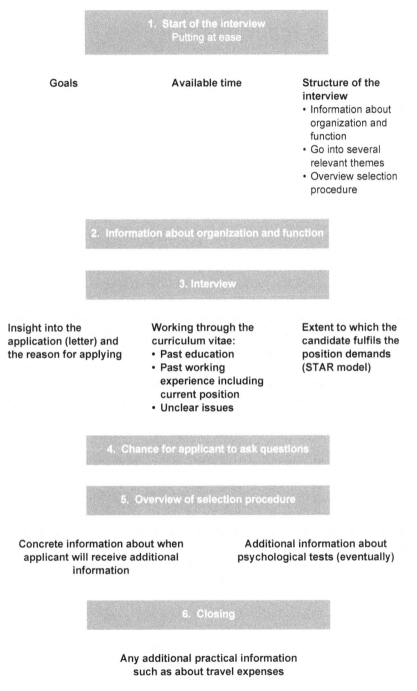

Figure 5.1 Overview of the selection interview

6 The job application interview

Practical example

Ken Klein, 32 years old, has worked in a small hotel since he graduated from hotel school. He has been with this hotel for eight years and now feels the need to change his working environment. He has been orientating himself to new possibilities for some time. One Saturday morning when he's looking at the newspaper advertisements, he notices a vacancy with Dinner Ltd. An Assistant F&B manager is sought 'due to one of our colleagues leaving'. When he reads the ad, Ken gets excited. This is his chance! After some discussion with his wife, he decides to answer the advertisement.

Writing the application letter is quite difficult, but once it is in the mail the period of tense waiting begins. Three weeks later the answer from Dinner Ltd arrives in the following letter:

Dear Mr Klein,

In response to your application for the function of Assistant F&B Manager, we would like to invite you for an interview next Wednesday at 10.00 hrs.

Included you will find some information about our company. If you would like more information about the function prior to the interview, please feel free to contact me.

With kind regards,

H. Haddock (Chairman of the Selection Committee)

Introduction

The application interview is actually comparable to a selling interview (see Chapter 10): the item that the applicant is selling is himself. As we live in a culture where modesty is more appreciated than telling others how good one is, some people still find it hard to sell themselves well. Another reason why people consider this difficult is because there is a lack of teaching of 'job application techniques' in most types of education. People who have been working in a company for many years and want to change jobs have perhaps forgotten their job application skills.

We will limit ourselves in this chapter to the *application interview*. This chapter is structured as follows: the importance of a good preparation for the application interview is shown. An overview of several often occurring questions is given. The skills that are important are then discussed and the chapter ends with a summarizing overview.

Preparation

After the initial excitement about the invitation for an interview has faded away, the following question quickly arises: 'What do I do now?' People are often rather nervous about the application interview: a definite performance has to be given in approximately 45 minutes. There is no chance for an improved version. Support from others is no longer possible. Moreover, the personal confrontation with the selector or selection committee often feels threatening. Applicants have to reveal themselves at such an interview, while the selector/selection committee remains in a safe and more powerful position.

Moreover, people often do not know exactly what to expect from an application interview. They sometimes do not know how to prepare themselves for it appropriately. This is a pity because thorough preparation is essential for good development of the conversation. The most important part of preparation is to think about the relationship between your personal capacities on the one hand and the requirements of the job for which you are applying on the other. This link should form the red thread through the entire conversation.

General advice

We first give some general advice about the preparation of the application interview:

1   Do not leave preparation to the last minute.
2   Try to orient yourself as well as possible. It is useful to form a clear picture of the organization. You can make use of annual reports, personnel magazines, etc. You may also call the company and ask for information. Points to take note of are:
•   What is the position of the job within the organization?
•   What does the company do exactly?
•   What is the hierarchical structure?

- What is the organizational culture?
- How is the organization doing? Are there any problems?
- How large is the organization?
- Who will be your colleagues?
  There are of course many other questions to be thought of. With each answer you can check whether or not you like the organization – the more it matches your own wishes the better.
3   Anticipate possible questions.
4   Make notes of the information you have collected. You can take these notes along to the application interview.
5   Try to imagine what kind of person the company would like to see in the job you are applying for.
6   Contact the people you would like as a reference if you haven't already done so when writing the application letter.

Questions that can be expected

The questions that can be expected usually cover several subjects: motivation, education, work experience, social background, personal characteristics, life experience, insight into the organization. Nine frequently asked questions are:

1   What attracts you about this position?
2   Why are you applying to us specifically?
3   What are your strong and your weak points?
4   How do you think you can compensate for your lack of experience?
5   What did you do after you finished your education?
6   How has the rest of your career been?
7   Why did you choose that type of education?
8   How would you solve a difference of opinion with your direct supervisor?
9   What is your style of leadership?

The answers to these questions should be logical and clear: good arguments are absolutely necessary.

At the end of the interview the selection committee often asks whether applicants have any questions of their own. It is important to have something to ask at this specific moment. By asking your own questions you show that you have thought about the job and clearly demonstrate your motivation and interest.

Skills in the job application interview

We now discuss several skills that can be used during an application interview. First, we will discuss the entry, listening, nonverbal skills and paralinguistic skills. Then we deal with a number of important verbal skills: arguing, positive formulation, thinking aloud, assertiveness, asking questions, and closing the interview.

The entry

The first blow is half the battle (Chaplin, Phillips, Brown, Clanton, & Stein, 2000): how you enter as an applicant is of great significance to the rest of the interview. The entry is so important because the first impressions of the selector/selection committee are often very influential (Dickson, Hargie, & Morrow, 1997; Millar & Gallagher, 1997; Whetzel & McDaniel, 1999). Whether an applicant will be chosen or not is often decided (sometimes unconsciously) early on in the interview. In the beginning phase an image is built of the applicant that will only change slightly during the remaining conversation. Reconsideration is not excluded, but selectors are inclined to look for facts to support their initial impressions. With this in mind it is clear why extra attention needs to be paid to the entry and essential factors include:

- neat grooming/clothing
- being there on time (not too early, certainly not too late)
- a firm handshake (dry not too warm hands)
- waiting to be seated until a seat is offered
- laying down your notebook with prepared questions on the table in front of you.

Listening

When a selection committee member is speaking, it is essential to listen carefully to what is said. This may sound like forcing an open door advice. However, there are applicants who are so nervous or so full of what they are going to say that they hardly hear any of the information they receive from the members of the selection committee. If you don't understand some information, you can ask for an explanation. However, in the first phase of the interview you shouldn't ask too many questions. Mainly you should concentrate on the information from the selection committee.

Nonverbal skills

The application interview is a means of getting information about the applicant for the selection committee. The committee members will therefore pay much attention during an interview to the content of the information an applicant is providing. They will also notice the applicant's nonverbal behaviour. Body posture, way of looking (eye contact) and gestures all influence the impression being made.

You have an adequate *body posture* when you sit upright in your chair, relaxed, with your hands loosely resting on your lap or the table. A good *sitting position* will contribute to a positive impression on the selection committee. A slouching applicant looks weak and unmotivated, while a rigid, upright posture and wiggling feet give a nervous impression.

Eye contact is also a relevant aspect of nonverbal behaviour. When members of the committee are speaking, the applicant should look at them in a friendly manner. When answering as the applicant, look at the different members occasionally.

Gestures are an important part of nonverbal behaviour. These can enforce words or enliven a story. People who make many gestures should generally try not to overdo it during an application interview as too many gestures quickly give a nervous impression. People who never or hardly ever make gestures can try to give a more lively impression by making a few gestures. However, one has to be careful that this doesn't give an unnatural impression.

Paralinguistic skills

Paralinguistic skills have to do with your style of speech. They are pre-requisites in order to be able to handle verbal skills such as arguing and formulating that will be discussed below. Attention should be paid to articulation, vocal volume and tone.

It is essential that you *speak clearly* and that you can be heard well during an application interview. For good intelligibility it is very important to have a *clear articulation*. This means clearly saying all the words and syllables of which these words consist. An unintelligible mumbling applicant will often annoy the selection committee.

A second aspect that influences intelligibility is *vocal volume*. Someone who speaks too loudly can make a rude impression. Someone who speaks too softly often gives a shy and insecure impression.

Third, *the tone* of voice influences the clarity of what is said. A confident, enthusiastic tone often makes the best impression on a selection committee.

We will now deal with a number of verbal skills.

Arguing

It is important during the application interview that your answers are consistent and answer the question being asked. You should try to give arguments as to why you are the best applicant for this job. Questions where clear arguing is necessary often start with 'Why'. Examples include: 'Why do you actually want to change jobs?' 'Why have you taken so much longer to complete your studies than the usual norm?' In response to these kinds of questions it is important that the answer:

- is relevant to the function
- is direct
- includes logic
- is concrete
- is structured.

An answer is relevant when its content matches the requirements of the job. When for example applicants are asked why they have applied for the position of project manager, it is better to give some detailed information about experience working for the previous company rather than just saying that one is bored with the current position.

Your answer also has to be logical and concrete. When you have said at the beginning of the conversation that it seems attractive to you to work in a team and a little later you say that during your education you preferred to work alone than with a fellow student, then logic is not to be found.

Finally, you should make sure that your answer is structured and that you don't jump from one subject to another. This does not lead to clarity for members of the selection committee.

Positive formulation

As an applicant you are trying to give a good impression of yourself during the interview. You want to get the job you are applying for and that can only be achieved by convincing the members of the selection committee that you are the most qualified person for that position and that you have all the skills needed for the job. Formulating in a positive manner enhances a positive self-presentation. Below we provide several examples of questions and how you can present some negative points in a positive manner:

1 The committee asks why you took longer to finish your education than the norm. Do not answer that it was not so easy in the beginning and that your studies didn't interest you as much as you had expected or that during your studies you got fed up with all the work and went off and did something else for a while. Formulate your answer positively and show that you had a wide range of interests. Maybe you did some charity work alongside your studies or you led an active student association life.

2 As an out-of-work recent graduate the committee asks you a question about what you have done in the period after your graduation and preceding the interview. Don't say that it is so hard to get a job because there is so little on offer, but indicate that you have been actively

searching for a job, or that you have done some voluntary work, or that you have followed some extra courses. Show clearly that you have not been sitting passively at home waiting till something was offered to you, but that you have used your initiative.

3   You are asked why you applied to this company in particular. Don't say that you find it important to have a job because you finally want to put into practice all the learned theory and that incidentally this company has a position on offer that fits in with your studies perfectly. Show that from the information you have gathered it is evident (indicating you have done some research) that the organization matches your own style, atmosphere or ideology, preference, ambition or vision, and that therefore it seems attractive for you to work here. Alternatively indicate that you have heard from relatives or family that the company has a favourable working climate where personal effort and initiative are noted and valued.

These examples are not meant to obscure the truth or to say what the selectors want to hear – what you don't mean you should not say – but they are meant to give you an idea of how you might formulate what you want to say in the most positive manner.

Thinking aloud

During an application interview you will always be confronted by unexpected questions, even though you have prepared yourself thoroughly. These unexpected questions are sometimes so tricky that you don't know the answer straightaway. The silence that follows can make you feel uneasy and as an applicant you may sometimes have difficulties in thinking clearly. The consequence may be that you quickly just say something in order to answer the question or you might not find an answer at all. A silence like this can also raise doubts in the selectors. They don't know why the applicant is silent for such a long time or what is going through his mind. Doesn't he have an answer to the question? Doesn't he have an opinion regarding the question asked? Is he afraid to answer? Is he unable to answer because the subject is too heavy? Doesn't he want to answer because he finds the question too personal? Therefore they don't know exactly how to interpret the silence. This leads to an unclear situation which is not favourable to the rest of the conversation.

In order to avoid such an uncomfortable situation, you would do better to indicate that you find it difficult to answer the question immediately and would like to think it over: for example, 'Oh . . ., that is a difficult question. I will have to think about it . . .' The selectors then know what is going on in your head and will give you time and space to think about the question. By thinking aloud you avoid uncomfortable silences and prevent your thought processes from getting blocked.

Assertiveness

It can occur during an application interview that the selector asks a question that is completely irrelevant to the job, or which you find too personal, and would rather not answer. An ethical committee of the Ministry of Social Affairs in the Netherlands, which used to be involved with creating legal rules and regulations for selection procedures, has set up several rules for selection committees. Here are examples of questions that this committee does not allow:

- *Marital status*: 'Are you married or single? Divorced? Engaged? Living together? Are you still in contact with your previous partner?'
- *Children*: 'Do your children still live at home? Who takes care of them? Are you planning to have more children?'
- *Legal record*: 'Have you ever been arrested or convicted? Have you ever been in prison?'
- *Military service*: 'What leave are you on? In which unit did you serve?'
- *Age*: 'You must be older than . . . aren't you?'
- *Living situation*: 'Do you have your own house or do you rent it?'

The committee mentioned above has noted that subjects such as psychiatric or legal involvement should not play a role in any part of the selection procedure; neither should marital status or sexual inclination. This does not mean that each and every selection committee will abide by the rules. If you don't want to answer a certain question then you can react assertively by asking in the first place what the relevance of the question is to the job. Many applicants find this difficult because one depends on the selectors to get the job, which is why applicants often quickly answer any questions asked. One prefers to ignore the fact that it is not 'legal' and answer anyway in order not to give up on a chance of getting a job. Sometimes this is better because a refusal to answer often gives a more negative impression than a short and businesslike reflection of the truth. However, if you really cannot see the relevance of the question to the function, say so in a friendly manner and also indicate why you don't see the relevance.

Asking questions and the end of the interview

In the ending phase of the interview the applicant will get the opportunity to ask questions. The purpose for the selectors here is to check whether everything is clear and to give the applicant the chance to pose questions on relevant topics which have not come up yet. Applicants often find it difficult to ask questions themselves because they don't have any questions or they are afraid of sounding stupid or impudent. However, in general it is important to ask a few questions. Usually it is appreciated and shows interest and motivation. It is also essential that you prepare adequately for this. Check for yourself what is unclear and what you would like to know. It is useful to note down the questions and take them along to the interview. When the selector gives you a chance to ask questions, you can easily get out your list. Try then to get a clear answer. Questions that can be asked include:

- How did the vacancy occur?
- Whom will I be working with?
- What are the labour conditions (training opportunities, holiday arrangements, etc.)?

If you have come to the conclusion during the interview that you are not interested in the position, for whatever reason, then you may choose to say this straightaway. You can also choose to sleep on it for a night and inform the committee later of your negative decision. In the ending phase the selection committee may want to know some practicalities. Questions you may prepare for include:

- When would you be able to start?
- Are you currently applying for other jobs?
- Do you object to research into your antecedents?

With these questions you would do best to answer truthfully. If you have other interviews running, you can easily say that as well. This ensures clarity and in some cases might even enhance the interest of the selection committee.

The result of the interview is hardly ever revealed immediately. The chairman will explain the remaining procedures (if this has not been done already) and tell you whether you should expect a written answer or a phone call. Usually the chairman will also announce when this should be expected. If the procedure remains unclear, ask about it yourself. It is always nice to know when to expect an answer. When the conversation has ended, thank the members of the selection committee for the interview and say goodbye.

Figure 6.1 gives an overview of the job application interview.

Selection committee	Applicant
0. Preparation: making an interview scheme (see Chapter 4)	0. Linking of own capacities to the job demands, preparing answers to difficult questions
1. Putting at ease	1. Introduce oneself, sitting down quietly
2. Introduction: indicate goal, time, structure	2. Listening, nonverbal skills: body posture, eye contact
3. Giving information about the organization and function	3. Listening, nonverbal skills: sitting position, eye contact

4. • Interview: explanation of letter and motivation
• Working through the résumé:
  (a) the education
  (b) past working experience
  (c) unclear issues
• Extent to which an applicant meets the job demands
	4. Nonverbal skills: gestures
	Paralinguistic skills: articulation, vocal volume, tone
	Arguing
	Positive formulation
	Thinking aloud
	Assertiveness

5. Giving chance to ask questions	5. Asking own questions
6. Giving an overview of the remaining procedure	6. Listening, asking questions in case of unclarity
7. Ending conversation	7. Thanking for the interview

Figure 6.1 Overview of the job application interview

7 The performance evaluation interview

Practical example

At Dinner Ltd each employee has an annual performance evaluation interview. The general goal of such an evaluation interview is to attune the interests of the organization and the employees in an optimal manner. Not only is the performance of an employee discussed, but the employee can also bring the functioning of a manager or colleague into the discussion. So there is a two-way traffic. This interview does not have any direct consequences for a potential promotion or on wages.

Every other year the employees at Dinner Ltd have an appraisal interview. In contrast to the performance evaluation we have here a one-way interview: the manager now evaluates the performance of the employee, which can have consequences for a promotion and salary increase.

At Dinner Ltd the performance evaluation interviews are held in December. Each department head has these interviews with their respective employees. For Managing Director Freddy Fortune, this means he will have interviews with Jenny Jacobson, the Secretary, with Charlotte Cohen from Finance and Administration, with Chef Bert Berman and with F&B Manager Harry Haddock. The dates when the interviews are to be held are arranged about a month in advance. Both parties involved are asked to suggest several points for the agenda.

In particular the interview with Charlotte Cohen seems as if it may be a difficult one. While Freddy believes that Charlotte puts much effort into her work, he also has some points of criticism: he feels that Charlotte takes too long to prepare proposals and that she often leaves off some essential elements from the final bills. For example, with the last catering assignment, a New Year's reception for the Ministry of Justice, she had estimated the number of necessary part-time personnel too low, with the result that the extra costs for personnel could not be billed. This is only one example of many similar instances: in general Charlotte is not accurate enough.

Charlotte also has some points that she want to discuss. In the first place it has been a while since she has been able to take a course in order to improve her own skills. In the second place she thinks that lately there has been too little consultation regarding several new assignments. Freddy is constantly on the road and hardly ever reachable. Because of this she is often responsible for making some very important decisions, which takes up so much of her energy that she therefore makes mistakes with the proposals.

Introduction

In this chapter first we place the performance evaluation interview within the framework of personnel management. We also discuss the most important differences between the performance evaluation and the appraisal interview. Next we discuss the goal of the performance evaluation interview and a number of conditions it has to fulfil, in order to be able to set up a system of performance evaluation interviews within the organization. We then look at the preparation phase of the performance evaluation interview and the different roles one should try to integrate. Although the performance evaluation differs from the appraisal interview, this does not mean that the manager should not evaluate the behaviour of the employee. Some of the most common evaluation mistakes are then discussed. Finally we examine a concrete model with the skills to be used for staging a performance evaluation interview. The summary of the interview model closes this chapter.

The performance evaluation interview within the framework of personnel management

In the performance evaluation both the interests of the company and the individual employee play a role. These interests cannot be viewed separately (Veen, 1991):

> The person will strive to adjust the organization in such a way that his needs and values, which he tries to satisfy through the organization, are dealt with as much as possible. The organization will strive to adjust the behaviour of the individual in such a way that this will be profitable for the organization (translation by the authors of this book).

For both the organization and the individual employee it is of great importance that the performance evaluation provides the possibility to talk in a pleasant and significant way that satisfies the needs of both parties.

In many organizations performance evaluation interviews are a new topic, although decades of literature have been mentioning this phenomenon. For example, the theme was discussed at a conference of the Dutch Association for Labor and Organizational Psychology in 1976. At this conference it was noted that an evaluation system which barely closes off a previous period and does not explicitly allow a future perspective with

Table 7.1 Differences between performance evaluation interview and appraisal interview

Performance evaluation interview	Appraisal interview
Work behaviour and work relationships are the focal points. How did it go in the past period? What went right, what went less right? In the interview one searches for the causes of problems and ways of solving them. There are explicitly no consequences for wages or promotion involved in this interview.	In this interview the consequences of a prior appraisal interview are the focal point. The employee is confronted with a judgement. Sometimes there are direct consequences for promotion and wage adaptations.
Manager and employee are talking.	Manager is primarily doing the talking.
Manager and employee make agreements together.	The manager takes the decisions.

regard to the development of the individual and the task, misses essential aspects for the motivation of the person to be evaluated. Until that time employees would only occasionally be evaluated. The management then expressed their thoughts about the achievements of the employee, about possibilities for further development and the consequences for wage levels. Research has shown that these kinds of interviews, also taking into consideration the changing opinions of society about how people should work with others, were often perceived as not being functional. At the same conference several principles were discussed for a more human evaluation system and included:

- more emphasis on the equality of the conversation parties
- more emphasis on the tasks than on the person
- more emphasis on the future than on the past.

These principles also led to a plea for the implementation of different types of interviews. A distinction was made between the performance evaluation interview on the one hand and the appraisal interview on the other. Some important differences are listed in Table 7.1.

The performance evaluation interview should be part of a larger evaluation system within personnel policy. When a general personnel policy values the involvement of employees with issues that concern them and the improvement of cooperation between managers and employees, the performance evaluation interview is an important tool. However, having performance evaluation interviews is of little use unless these interviews are part of an integral personnel policy. To illustrate: an employee says in a performance evaluation interview that he would like to have more responsibilities and the manager also believes this would be a positive development. This wish then has to be transformed into concrete action, for example, by following a course (training policy) or the attaining of a higher position (promotion policy).

Goal and conditions

The general goal of the performance evaluation interview is to bring the interests of the organization and the employee in line with each other. In specific terms this interview is directed at the improvement of both the motivation and work results of the employee, as well as the cooperation between employee and manager and between employee and other colleagues. It is an often reoccurring interview in which the work itself, the work atmosphere, the work performance and the work circumstances are discussed and decisions are made regarding observed problems. Finally, this interview should lead to agreements in order to resolve problems or to establish certain aspects of improvement.

In order to be able to reach these goals certain conditions should be fulfilled. These conditions have regard to the implementation of such a system of performance evaluation interviews in an organization. First, both the employees and managers need to be involved in setting up and introducing the interviews and be able to understand the importance of them for themselves as well as for the organization. Second, it should be clear for all those involved how the data will be used. When this clarity is missing, the result is that employees are on their guard during the interview because of the possible consequences for their salary or career. Third, one has to keep in mind that holding performance evaluation interviews demands a high degree of managerial social skills. Finally, each organization has a 'social climate' and it is of importance to check whether this climate is of such a nature that it is 'ready' for the implementation of a system of performance evaluation interviews.

Preparation

In order be able to hold the performance evaluation interview in an efficient way, good preparation by both partners is necessary. We assume that both are aware of the goal of performance evaluation interview. When the manager and employee have already had such an interview before, then they both have a (short) report of the agreements that were made in that interview.

If it is the first performance evaluation interview, the manager needs to have to hand a job description or a file with notes about the past period. An appointment needs to be set up with the employee involved. The general goal is to discuss together how the employee has performed over the past period. Employees are asked in advance what points they would especially like to have discussed during the interview. This especially involves mentioning points that are not going well or could be improved. These points could concern the task, personal aspects of the employee, cooperation with others or cooperation with the manager. It may be useful to jot down these points on paper for use as a memory aid during the interview.

Roles

The manager has the role of interview leader: that is to say he or she regulates the interview and makes sure the opinion of the employee is heard. By being open-minded about the points the employee brings forward, the manager stimulates expression of views and thoughts regarding the job. The manager also has to fulfil the role of 'expert' and on some issues is better able to come up with possible solutions for the diagnosed problem because of their expertise. In reality the manager should be able to fulfil both the leader and expert role. The tone of the interview should be businesslike and focused on cooperation: solving problems together is the focal point.

Errors of judgement

During preparation for the interview the manager forms an opinion over a longer time period. When judging someone's performance and predicting someone's capabilities, mistakes might be made. Most of us are not aware of these mistakes at all. We have a tendency, for example, to observe the things that we expect to see. When we dislike somebody we may see the negative sides much more than the positive sides. Furthermore, there is a stubborn bias that is often implicitly taken into account when judging someone, such as: Scottish people are stupid, women cannot drive a car, etc. We may use such prejudices in order not to have to adjust our opinions. It is easier for us to place people in little boxes and keep them there. This error of judgement is also typified as 'labelling'. You label someone and then do not check to see if the person has changed – you just look at the label. We now discuss some other often occurring errors of judgement.

Avoiding extreme judgements

People who have to evaluate others often avoid extreme judgements; they limit themselves to the middle of the rating scale. This is the reason why there is little differentiation (Roe & Daniels, 1984). An explanation for the tendency to avoid low judgement is that one is scared to deliver bad news (see Chapter 10). It is also possible that extreme negative judgements are not considered to be useful to motivate an employee. A final explanation for the tendency to avoid extreme positive or negative judgements is that it makes it harder to criticize the particular employee in the future.

Leniency

By leniency we mean an evaluation that is too positive. This mistake often occurs in organizations where the relationships between managers and employees are more amicable than hierarchical. The bilateral dependency is therefore greater so the evaluations should not be too negative, otherwise the motivation and atmosphere in the workplace are endangered.

Halo effect

The halo effect means that a positive aspect of a person overshadows all other aspects. Therefore one positive aspect becomes the reason that a person is evaluated positively overall: for example, a project manager who is good at dealing with the executors is therefore also evaluated positively with regard to the administration process and priority setting at work, even though he might be functioning in a mediocre manner in these areas.

Horn effect

The horn effect is the opposite of the halo effect when, for example, the evaluator in general has a negative judgement of the employee based on one aspect only. A secretary who does not fill in the office agenda neatly is evaluated on other aspects more negatively than she deserves.

Psychologizing

Psychologizing means that a comment is made about a person's character based on one aspect of his functioning. For example, when an employee has difficulties in setting priorities it may be said that he feels insecure and is not able to work independently. Often a first result of 'psychologizing' is that the employee is labelled in a certain way. When the manager 'psychologizes' in an interview (e.g. 'You are the dependent type, anyway') it often results in the employee getting irritable. Moreover such judgements are not concrete and usually do not give the opportunity for positive improvement in the employee's behaviour.

Preventing mistakes

There are numerous mistakes that can be made unconsciously. The evaluation should therefore be made very carefully. The following rules of thumb can help to minimize such mistakes.

- Evaluate over a longer period so that individual incidents are not the only items evaluated.
- Evaluate according to the function.

- Do not compare with a colleague who has a different function.
- Try to understand your own evaluation mistakes. Be aware of them, so you can reduce some of them.
- Note down the facts as much as possible during the evaluation period according to concrete behaviour and achievements.

The performance evaluation interview model

We now outline the interview model, which is composed of four parts: the start of the interview, composition of the agenda, discussion of the subjects, and ending the interview.

Start of the interview

The manager opens the interview with a short summary of its goal and indicates how long it will last (see p. 9).

> In the interview at Dinner Ltd between Freddy Fortune and Charlotte Cohen, Freddy says: 'As you know the goal of this performance evaluation interview is to discuss what has happened in the past period and how we are going to tackle eventual problems in the forthcoming period. We now have an hour for this.'
>   Furthermore he indicates the structure of the conversation and refers to its preparation: 'We had agreed that we would both think about certain subjects that we wanted to discuss. I suggest we start by making a list of the subjects to be discussed. You can start with your points, then I will mention my own points. Next we can discuss each point one by one. Finally, I would like to list all the agreements we will have made for the coming period. Do you agree with this?'

Composition of the agenda

It has been agreed upon beforehand that both manager and employee will note down on paper the points they want to discuss in the interview. The manager lists these points at the beginning of the interview in cooperation with the employee. It is best if both parties try to characterize each of the points by a keyword. Sometimes a short explanation is needed. The manager has to avoid the type of listing that goes into detail on the various points. It has to be clear that it only involves making the agenda.

> Freddy and Charlotte arrive at the phase of the agenda points.
> *Charlotte's points*:
> - new course
> - too little discussion about new catering assignments.

Freddy's points:
- strong dedication
- long preparation proposals
- mistakes in bills.

Discussion of the agenda points

Employee's discussion points

As agreed, the manager allows the employee to speak first. 'About the first point you mentioned, "new course", can you please explain what you mean by that?' While the employee explains this point, the listening skills are especially important: attentive behaviour, asking questions, paraphrasing, reflection of feelings and concreteness.

If it has been made clear what the nature of the problem is and how the employee views it, the manager then gives his own opinion. The fact that he shows understanding for the viewpoint of the employee does not necessarily mean that he agrees with it at all times. He should also be able clearly to state his own opinion. However, before he starts to discuss the aspects that he disagrees with, he indicates on which points he does agree. Then for each point a concrete solution is sought together.

It can also occur that the employee criticizes the manager. This will be the case, for example, when Freddy and Charlotte discuss the second point.

> Charlotte believes there is too little discussion regarding new catering assignments and that Freddy is not available enough. 'To be honest, Freddy, I think we talk too little about the new assignments. The reason is you are out much of the time and I don't know where to reach you.'

Reacting to criticism (see p. 30) is an important skill in a performance evaluation interview. Many people are inclined to regard criticism as a direct personal attack. They then try to defend themselves by attacking the other person in return, thus producing negative results. Criticism can often help in getting things sorted out and may form a basis for improving cooperation. In the first place it is essential that the manager listens quietly and checks with himself whether he understands the other person's criticism. When he has heard out the criticism, several different approaches are possible. In the first place he can partly or totally agree with the criticism. In this case he can agree with the other person and indicate how he is going to try and change his behaviour:

> Freddy Fortune could, for example, say: 'Yes indeed, I have been away quite often lately and I can imagine that has caused you to be over-

loaded. Maybe we should make an agreement for the coming period that we see each other for sure at least once a week at a fixed time.'

It is also possible that he totally or partly disagrees with the criticism. He then can (again) paraphrase what the employee has said and indicate his opinion about it. Next he can try to come to an agreement on this issue, maybe by making a compromise.

Sometimes the employee may be angry about something that has happened in the organization or angry with the manager himself. Being able to *react in an appropriate manner to anger* is an important skill for the manager. In the first place he has to keep in mind that the interview is of a functional, businesslike character. He can cope with emotions such as anger by dealing with them in a functional way. He can do so by asking for concreteness and by trying to find out as much as possible about the exact cause of the anger: 'Can you indicate what you exactly mean by "all the mess"? Can you give a concrete example?'

Sometimes it is necessary briefly to reflect the feelings of anger: 'I can imagine that you are angry. Shall we now try to look at this case peacefully so that we can find out in the best way possible what the reason for your anger is so we can do something about it?'

When the employee has had a chance to express his reasons for being angry, the manager can paraphrase: 'I understand that according to you the personnel department does not want to show compassion for your situation.' Then he may reflect his own point of view about it. Maybe the employee has also had a part in the development of the problems. However, it is not wise to bring this up too quickly; the danger exists that this will make the situation explode. Finally, the manager should try to make a concrete agreement in order to find a solution for the cause of the anger. When employees have brought up all their points, the manager checks whether all the issues have now been dealt with: 'Are there any other points that you would like to discuss at this moment?' At the end of this stage the manager may turn to his own points of discussion.

Manager's discussion points

Before discussing any possible problems, the manager starts by giving positive feedback. He might have the inclination to start immediately with the discussion of things that are not going well. However, receiving 'support' has a positive influence on the motivation and health of employees (Argyle, 1995). That is why it is important that the manager expresses the value of the positive aspects of the employee's functioning in concrete terms.

In the following example the positive feedback relates to the concrete actions of a task: 'In general it has come to my notice that you work very hard. You are usually one of the first people to come in and one of the last ones to leave!'

Besides positive feedback, the manager also sometimes needs to criticize (see p. 26). When giving criticism the manager should try to be as concrete as possible, so instead of saying 'You make mistakes all the time with personnel estimations' he could say 'With assignment X you made a mistake in the estimation of the amount of part-time personnel that were needed.'

It has to be clear that the manager does not give a negative judgement of the person as a whole, but that he has a remark to make regarding specific behaviour in relation to the functioning of the employee. Criticizing is not easy. In the first place the manager could be scared of hurting the other person's feelings. In the second place, the relationship with the employee could be damaged if the manager says something negative about him. However, an irritable situation can be created if the manager always swallows his criticism. Irritation in a working situation can influence both the functioning of the manager and the employee in a negative way. It is important, therefore, to be open, honest and clear when giving criticism:

> The tone should thus be businesslike (assertive), not aggressive: 'I'm really fed up with this . . .', but also not sub-assertive: 'Well, I really find it difficult to tell you this, but . . .' It is better to say: 'According to me the preparation time for projects is too long. I really want to discuss with you what the reasons are for this and how we can improve the situation.'

When discussing points, about which some decisions were taken in the previous performance evaluation interview, the manager could start by giving an overview of these points: 'We agreed last time that you would write a monthly short report about the complaints that have come into your department. Since then I have been receiving the reports neatly on time. However the information is not always very clear.' In this example we see that the manager starts with positive feedback. Then he indicates a concrete point for improvement.

When the criticism is about a new point the manager first indicates the problem: for example, 'It occurs quite often that people make a phone call to you and I cannot reach you. It is very difficult for me to indicate to these people where and when they *can* reach you.'

It is important to make sure that the employee recognizes the problem: 'Can you see that this is difficult for me?'

Next the manager asks the employee whether he has any ideas for improvement of his own: 'Do you have any suggestions as to how we can arrange this better in the future?' If the manager agrees with the employee's solution, he can then move on to formulation of the agreement to be made.

If he has a different idea, he should paraphrase the employee's proposal and then give his own opinion.

On all points of discussion the manager and employee are working towards concrete agreements for the coming period. These agreements are formulated as clearly as possible: for example, 'We agree that we will meet more often, namely once a week. Hopefully this will take some pressure off you, since you won't have to take difficult decisions all by yourself.' Finally the manager checks whether the employee agrees with this formulation.

Ending the interview

At the end of the interview the manager first summarizes the agreements made and asks the employee's opinion about them. Afterwards some attention may be paid to the performance evaluation interview itself. When an employee has a performance evaluation interview for the first time, this subject gets more attention than if it is a routine event. The purpose of the interview is mentioned again: 'The purpose of this interview was to discuss what we both think of your functioning and our cooperation.'

Next the manager asks whether the interview has met the expectations of the employee: 'Are you satisfied with the way we reached the agreements?' The manager also explicitly asks the opinion of the employee about the interview: 'Do you think it has been a useful interview?'

Finally the manager gives his own judgement of the interview. He closes off by making appointments concerning the written report of the interview and possibly setting the next interview with the employee. (See Figure 7.1 for an overview of the performance evaluation interview.)

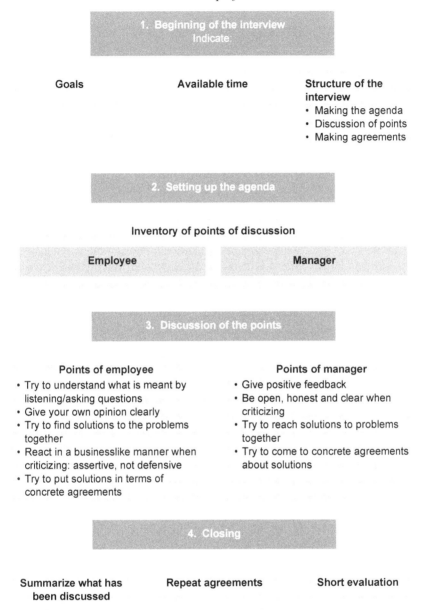

1. Beginning of the interview
Indicate:

Goals

Available time

Structure of the interview
- Making the agenda
- Discussion of points
- Making agreements

2. Setting up the agenda

Inventory of points of discussion

Employee

Manager

3. Discussion of the points

Points of employee
- Try to understand what is meant by listening/asking questions
- Give your own opinion clearly
- Try to find solutions to the problems together
- React in a businesslike manner when criticizing: assertive, not defensive
- Try to put solutions in terms of concrete agreements

Points of manager
- Give positive feedback
- Be open, honest and clear when criticizing
- Try to reach solutions to problems together
- Try to come to concrete agreements about solutions

4. Closing

Summarize what has been discussed

Repeat agreements

Short evaluation

Figure 7.1 Overview of the performance evaluation interview

8   The personal problems interview

Practical example

F&B Manager Harry Haddock has been under the impression that one of his headwaiters, Alex Armstrong, is not functioning as well as usual. Alex looks tired, and is often absent-minded during meetings. Remarks from Alex's team of waiters have made it clear that Alex has been rather irritable. For example, if the guests have to wait a little longer than usual, Alex gets into a state, even if the guests haven't noticed the delay. Due to this, Alex's relationship with his team is deteriorating. Harry is wondering what's wrong. Things cannot go on like this, something has to be done. Harry is not looking forward to talking with Alex. He knows Alex is very touchy and very private when it comes to personal matters. Nevertheless, he decides to invite Alex for a personal interview. Alex arrives at the arranged time.

Introduction

In the practical example above we see that Harry Haddock is under the impression that Alex Armstrong might be having some personal problems that are affecting his work. The example ends at the moment when Harry is about to undertake a special and difficult part of his job as manager: conducting a conversation with an employee about (suspected) personal problems. In our example Harry Haddock initiated this conversation, which is difficult to do since he will have to state his reasons. Whether Alex wants this interview remains to be seen.

If employees in an organization experience personal problems, they will not usually flaunt them. We are not suggesting they should. Everyone has problems and should be able to decide for themselves whether and with whom they choose to discuss them. Therefore we make a clear distinction between personal problems that do not affect work and those that do (or seem to). In the latter case it might be in the interests of both employee and organization to have an opportunity openly to discuss personal problems. Often the person in charge should take the initiative for such a discussion.

Sometimes, however, employees will voluntarily approach either their manager or a colleague.

Our aim in this chapter is to present an interview model which managers can use in personal problem interviews. First we will compare two styles of dialogue: the *diagnosis-prescription model* and the *cooperation model* (Lang & Van der Molen, 2003). We also indicate our preference for the cooperation model. The choice of dialogue model that can be used in conducting an interview or a series of interviews is then discussed. Here we identify two phases: *problem clarification* and *action planning*. In both phases there are several goals for both manager and employee. We also examine the communication skills necessary to achieve these goals, and a general strategy for development of an action plan. We give attention to the skill of *giving advice* and under the same heading we deal with *referral*. If there are serious psychological problems it is advisable to refer the employee to a psychologist or psychiatrist. We finish with a *summary* of the dialogue model.

Diagnosis-prescription model versus cooperation model

We now discuss two styles that the manager can use in the personal problems interview. In order to explain both styles we make use of our practical example. The following two fragments of dialogue illustrate both styles:

Fragment 1

1   HARRY: Alex, I've asked you in for a chat, because I have a feeling your work's not going well. Do you have any thoughts about this?
    ALEX: [a bit surprised] What do you mean by not going well?
2   HARRY: Come on Alex, don't tell me you haven't noticed. But if you insist, I'll give you some examples. During our last meeting I noticed you weren't as involved as usual, as if your mind was somewhere else. And then the waiters in the team tell me you're unreasonably short with them. Well, it's made me think. I could be wrong, but I thought there might be a problem.
    ALEX: Yeah, I see what you mean. It's true, I've done better.
3   HARRY: Has anything happened here?
    ALEX: No, nothing special, although we are behind schedule.
4   HARRY: True, and that's a nuisance, but it's no reason to walk around with a long face.
    ALEX: I guess not.
5   HARRY: So, has anything happened between you and one of the waiters, or something else here at work?
    ALEX: No, no, not that I know . . .
6   HARRY: Well, then that's not it. [looks pensive]
    ALEX: [waits]
7   HARRY: Hmm, let's see, are you having more trouble concentrating than before?

ALEX: No, not really.
8   HARRY: Everything all right at home, Alex?
ALEX: Sure, everything's fine.

The conversation continues along the same lines: Harry asks the questions, Alex gives short answers and waits for the next question. Harry tries to find out why Alex is not functioning well, but Alex does not seem to cooperate. The (implicit) idea behind Harry's behaviour is that the easiest way to find the true cause of a problem is to ask a lot of questions. Then, it is thought, sound advice can be given. This dialogue model is called the *diagnosis-prescription model*. Such a dialogue is very similar to a conversation with a (conventional) physician: he asks a lot of questions, makes a diagnosis and writes out a prescription.

This kind of conversation is not always doomed to fail. In some cases the nature and cause of the problem can thus be found. Whether a solution can be found is another matter. There are, however, some serious drawbacks to this method when dealing with personal problems. First, the person experiencing personal problems cannot always pinpoint the cause. Usually there are several causes. Second, during such a conversation it is very difficult to talk about problems in one's own way and order. In the fragment above we see Alex more or less submissively answering the question and waiting for the next one. A consequence of this direct question method (see p. 16) is the difficulty in establishing a relationship of trust. We see Alex answering questions, usually in the negative, but there is no space or attention for him to come forward with things he may find very difficult to talk about. Thus the diagnosis-prescription model makes it easy for the other person to remain silent about difficult subjects.

The diagnosis-prescription model has certain disadvantages. Is there another method? Let's have a look at the next fragment, in which Harry uses the *cooperation model*:

Fragment 2
1   HARRY: Alex, I've asked you in for a chat because I have the feeling your work's not going well. At meetings for instance you seem to be absent-minded, and from the waiters in your team I hear you can be very hard on them. I'm worried about it, and I'd like us to talk about it. What do you think?
ALEX: [somewhat hesitant] Uh, . . . yes it's not going that well.
2   HARRY: I see you're hesitating. First, anything said here is just between you and me. And of course there's no need to tell me things you don't want to. Now, I have one hour; I would like to see it we can find out together what the problem is. Then we'll see if we can come up with some solutions. What do you think?
ALEX: [a little less hesitant] Sure, sounds like a good idea . . .
3   HARRY: Right. Now, as I said, I'd like to hear what you think of it.

ALEX: Well, you're right about me being absent-minded during meetings.

4   HARRY: Hmm, hmm. [looks at Alex questioningly]

ALEX: It's not that I'm not interested, I am, it's just that I'm having a hard time concentrating . . .

5   HARRY: Do you have any idea why?

ALEX: No, I'm not sure, there are all kinds of things.

6   HARRY: All kinds of things . . . Can you give me an example?

ALEX: Well, one of the things I'm wondering about is whether I should be moving on. I've been here for nine years now and I won't be getting any promotion . . .

7   HARRY: Go on . . .

ALEX: This is very difficult, you're not going to tell anyone are you?

8   HARRY: No, I'm not, I've already told you. But I understand it's difficult to talk about.

ALEX: Well, okay. This isn't really about getting promoted. Things aren't too good at home . . .

9   HARRY: What's wrong?

ALEX: I don't talk about it much, but my wife left me some time ago. She's got someone else . . .

10 HARRY: Good heavens, I'm sorry. How long has this been going on?

ALEX: Well, things hadn't been good for some time. About half a year ago she met this bloke and two months ago she moved in with her sister, because she wants to think things through. She doesn't know if she wants to stay with me or with that bloke. I feel so powerless.

11 HARRY: Hmm, I can imagine, you're just waiting to see what they come up with.

ALEX: Right. And I might as well tell you the rest of it: because I don't know what to do, I often go to the pub at night and I don't stop at three beers, if you know what I mean. Anyway, because of all this I'm not doing well at work and I know I'm too hard on the waiters but before I know it I've done it again . . .

Comparing the beginnings of the two fragments, we notice a difference right away. In the first fragment Harry, after a short introduction, immediately starts asking questions like a detective. In the second fragment he also tells Alex why he has invited him for this conversation, but he includes a couple of concrete examples, and he makes his own feelings clear: 'I'm worried about it . . .' This is, however, only half the basis needed for a cooperative relation. In order to establish the other half, Harry asks Alex explicitly if he wants to talk. Thus Alex is given the role of equal partner. You could say a contract is closed in which both parties agree to the conversation. In the second fragment we see Alex's hesitant reaction. This might be caused by Harry's last question: 'What do you think?' We do see him *admit* to the problem. Harry takes up Alex's hesitation and by acknowledging it (reaction 2) he shows understanding. But he does more than that. First he isolates this conversation from the rest of the company ('anything said here is just between you and me'). This is of importance to the confidentiality of the conversation. It is important to Alex, who might think that his story could spread through the company like wildfire. Then Harry tells Alex that he need not say anything unless he wants to. This makes Alex feel more at ease. Contrary to the events in the first fragment, there's no pressure on Alex. In the course of fragment 2 we see the positive effect this often has. If people do not try to force something out of you, but give you a chance to decide for yourself, you are often more willing to talk.

Prior to giving Alex a chance to talk, Harry makes a few things *clear*. First he mentions the amount of time available for this conversation. Of course there's always the possibility for further conversation should this be necessary. Then he explains to Alex *what kind* of conversation he would like this to be: 'I would like to see if we could find out together what the problem is. Then we'll see if we can come up with some solutions. What do you think?' Thus the basic outline of the conversation is marked. Alex knows what he's in for and is given another opportunity to make up his mind. We realize that not everybody will lose their inhibitions and open up after such a beginning, but the chance of cooperation increases if the other person feels he has an equal say in the matter and is taken *seriously*.

In fragment 2 (reactions 2 and 3) we see Alex's hesitation decreasing. He realizes he's not going to be put on the spot, but he decides to hold back a while longer. Once the basis for cooperation has been formed, Harry decides to begin with a general open question: 'I'd like to hear what you think of it' (action 3). He does not ask a series of questions in order to confirm his own suspicions, as in fragment 1, but he gives Alex some space.

Then Alex starts to talk, in bits and pieces. Harry restricts himself to listening, giving minimal encouragers (actions 4, 6, 7), asking open questions (actions 5, 9), one direct closed question (action 10), and showing understanding by means of reflection of feelings and paraphrasing content (actions 8, 10, 11). This causes Alex to lose some of his inhibitions and to talk more openly. In the end it becomes clear that his absent-mindedness and temper towards the waiters are caused by the situation at home.

This did not come out in the diagnosis-prescription conversation. Why not? Here we see a major difference between the diagnosis-prescription model and the cooperation model. In the diagnosis-prescription model the questions follow from Harry's preconceived ideas. In the cooperation model Harry connects as much as he can to what Alex says. Alex is given the opportunity to tell his *own story*.

In bringing our discussion of the second fragment to an end, we want to list the advantages of the cooperation model over the diagnosis-prescription model. First, the employee is encouraged to think *actively* about his problems. Thus an appeal is made to his *responsibility*. This results in a clearer view of the factors influencing the problems. Second, the relationship between manager and employee is more *confidential*. Third, there is no need to be as *directive* as in the diagnosis-prescription model, which makes it easier to listen to attentively.

Last but not least we want to mention some early scientific evidence supporting the cooperation model. Research (Lewin, 1958; Korsch & Negrete, 1972) shows that diagnosis-prescription advice is rarely taken. The same research shows that clarity and openness in the approach to the clients and their involvement in the recommendations led to higher rates of compliance.

It will be clear that we prefer the cooperation model for personal problem interviews with employees. We now proceed to show how to conduct such a conversation by presenting a dialogue model that can be seen as a specification of a more general cooperation model.

A dialogue model with communication skills

The dialogue model presented below is based on the work of Egan (2002). The function of the model is to arrange the various conversation goals with their respective methods, thus keeping a clear view of the situation. Before discussing the different phases of the model it should be stressed that dealing with someone else's personal problems is not easy. You should continually be aware of the fact that you are not a professional counsellor or psychotherapist. However, offering assistance within the workplace does have its advantages. For employees it might be easier to talk to a familiar person. Moreover, the manager knows part of the employee's situation. Especially when the problems result from work-related factors, knowledge of specific situations can be very useful. It is easier to understand the nature of the problem, and possibly simpler to take quick and concrete steps to eliminate the problem, for example, by mediating in a co-workers' conflict (see Chapter 15).

Phase 1: Problem clarification

The goal of the first phase in the personal problem interview is for both manager and employee to get a clear view of the problem. It is important for the manager to have a basic attitude of respect and acceptance of the employee as a person (Rogers, 1962). Since personal problems are not easily discussed, the beginning of the conversation is often hesitant and careful, as we have seen in fragment 2. It is the manager's task to clarify the procedure, and to invite the employee to talk. The manager listens, the employee notices he can talk freely or, if he'd rather, to stall for a bit.

When a relationship of confidence has been established, the manager will stimulate the employee to speak more freely. The main goal in this phase is to acquire a good view of the factors contributing to the problem, and of the thoughts, feelings and behaviour of the employee. At this point the goal is not making choices, establishing the exact nature of the problem or finding solutions. If it appears, in the course of conversation, that the employee is having problems at home and as a consequence is drinking heavily, as in our fictional case, the manager does not come forward with suggestions at this stage. His or her task is to listen carefully, but this is often not enough. He should also try to create some order in the conversation and to make vague statements concrete. The manager should try to search the employee's story for clues to solutions, which he keeps to himself for the time being.

Skills in Phase 1

In order to achieve the aforementioned goals, the manager needs regulating skills, such as situation clarification at the beginning of the conversation: for example, explaining why he invited the employee for an interview, indicating the amount of time available and the structure of the conversation; see Chapter 1 (Benjamin, 1987; Brammer & MacDonald, 1999). In addition, listening skills are of especial importance. In order to show the employee that he is interested, the manager has to make use of attentive behaviour, minimal encouragers, open and closed questions, paraphrases of content, reflection of feelings and concreteness (see Chapter 2). In order to give some structure to the story it is necessary to use summarizing skills (see p. 19).

Phase 2: Formulating an action plan

If phase 1 has led to clarification and clear description of the problems (whether through one or several conversations), we can move on to phase 2. In the action phase it is possible to work on solutions explicitly. Action in phase 2 means actively looking for a solution to the problem: in Alex's case 'How can we make sure your work does not suffer from your home situation?' or 'How can we make your home situation more tolerable?' In short, the goal in phase 2 is *to do* something about the problem.

How do we go about this? In our view the employee should decide which problem to tackle first. He should have the responsibility for this choice. If he is able to, he should also choose the means to achieve this goal. If he is not able to think of solutions himself, the manager should play an important role in this. Often people know *what* their problem is but they don't know *how* to change it. Even if they do *know* how to change it, it doesn't mean they can *bring about* this change. In short, in a number of cases the manager will have to *advise* the employee.

After making choices about goal and method in general, the manager will have to determine, after consultation with the employee, how to achieve the desired goal and which (new) behaviour is necessary. Supplying ways to deal with the problem is not enough, however. The manager will have to check what happens to the employee in attempts to deal with the problem. Is it working? There will have to be another conversation to evaluate the events. In the phase of problem clarification it may become clear that the manager is not equipped to deal with this problem. In the action phase he will then have to find possibilities for referral. For this he will need some knowledge of healthcare institutions.

In the next part we first describe a general strategy for the action phase. Second, we discuss the skill of giving advice.

General strategy in Phase 2

When the problems have become clear during the first phase, it is necessary to decide whether it is useful and possible to do something about them. We purposely say 'useful and possible'. In some cases it might *not* be *useful* to do anything. If all the employee wanted was to get something off his chest, one conversation might suffice. In other cases it may be *impossible* for the manager to do anything because the problem is too serious, as we have mentioned before.

What remains is a situation in which the two parties can think of a way to deal with the problem. We will limit ourselves to a discussion of a *general strategy* in dealing with problems. Of course, what exactly should be done depends on the specific content of the problem.

Steps in an action programme

We now briefly discuss nine separate steps of an action programme. Each step is illustrated by means of our fictional case.

Step 1: Problem clarification

In the preceding part we have said enough about problem clarification. Perhaps the manager will initiate an action programme, not needing further assistance, or the conversation has cleared the air and the existing situation is accepted. During their first conversation Harry summarizes Alex's problems and lists them as follows:

- Alex's wife is having a relationship with someone else and is trying to decide what to do.
- Alex feels abandoned and powerless.
- He drinks more than is good for him.
- Consequences: lack of concentration, worrying and short-tempered with the waiters.
- Separate problem: lack of promotion opportunity.

Step 2: Priorities

There often prove to be several problems or one problem of a complex nature. Which problem should be dealt with first? Manager and employee are not able to deal with all the problems at the same time. Therefore a certain order has to be established. It is not wise to begin with the 'worst' problem, since this is usually the most difficult to deal with. In order to promote self-confidence and the chance of success, it is advisable to start with a relatively simple problem:

> The problem Alex wants to tackle first is the situation at work. No matter how bad the situation at home, he does want to do well on the job. To him the most important part is his relationship with the waiters; meetings aren't that frequent. Although he wants to cut down on his drinking, this is not given priority: he drinks more than usual, but is not (yet) an alcoholic.

Step 3: Goals

Following the choice of problems, manager and employee should formulate goals that will lead to a reduction of those problems:

> The goal is to improve the relationship between Alex and his waiters. After all, they are working extra hard during peak hours and a bad relationship does not encourage them to continue working this hard.

Step 4: Means

The next step is to make a list of the means available to the employee to reach his goal. What can he do, what kind of help can he get? If there are several opportunities, it might help to list the pros and cons of each possibility:

> How does Alex improve the relationship with the waiters? During his conversation with Harry, Alex suggests the possibility of offering his apologies about his behaviour to the waiters during their break. The reasons for his behaviour he prefers to keep to himself.

Step 5: Criteria

Manager and employee decide together what results their actions should have in order to be called successful. These criteria are a further specification of the different goals that were set:

Harry and Alex decide that Alex will try to realize two things in the next week. First the relationship with the waiters will have to improve. This can be seen from the way he relates to the waiters; there's hardly any communication. Second, maybe less important from a personal, but more so from the business point of view, they will try to improve the routeing in order to make service faster.

Step 6: Execution

After discussing and organizing the action, the most important step is the execution of the plans. The employee will have to do something. Together they decide on the actual steps to be taken:

Alex will do what they agreed on the very next day. There's no time like the present.

Step 7: Evaluation

The employee returns for another conversation and discusses his experiences with the manager – what worked, what didn't, what else happened, to what extent, according to the criteria set in step 5, did he reach his goal? Also, what to do next, in view of the results:

One week later Harry and Alex have their next conversation. Alex has reached his goal on relationship improvement, since the waiters have accepted and appreciated Alex's apologies. However, he did not manage to keep his personal affairs out of it, since one of the waiters asked him what was wrong. He decided it might be better to tell them a bit more and mentioned his marital problems. He did not tell them about his drinking. They have not managed to improve the speed of the service because too many waiters called in sick last week. The important thing is that he and the waiters are getting along. But there is more to be done: Alex is still drinking heavily.

Step 8: A new start

Based on the evaluation the employee continues his course of action if necessary. It is also possible to tackle another problem. Depending on the progress of clarification, one of the first five steps can be taken again:

In another conversation Harry and Alex start dealing with the alcohol problem. Their goal is to reduce Alex's use of alcohol. They also discuss the lack of promotion opportunities. Although Harry does not see any immediate possibilities for Alex, they do decide he will take a refresher course in management skills.

Step 9: Conclusion

If the various goals have been reached, manager and employee can conclude their cooperation as far as personal problems are concerned.

> When Harry thinks Alex is working up to standard, the conversations about personal problems can be concluded. Of course Harry cannot make Alex's wife return: in view of the situation that would be best. Alex would not feel abandoned anymore, and he would not feel the need to go to the pub every night. However, Harry can help Alex to deal with his situation, whichever turn it takes.

Giving advice

An important skill in the action phase is giving advice. Although the cooperation model is based on cooperation between manager and employee, there are situations in which the manager has more skills to deal with certain aspects of a problem. In those cases the manager should take on a more directive role. If Alex Armstrong's only problem were choice of further education and Harry Haddock, with his more extensive experience, could give him sound advice, then he should. Advice should be given in plain terms, be well argued and succinct (see p. 22).

A special case of giving advice is *referral*. As we have said before, managers in organizations who conduct personal problems interviews should be well aware that they are not professional counsellors. If Alex Armstrong's drinking problem is a case of alcoholism, Harry Haddock should refer him first to his general practitioner, who in turn might refer him to a psychologist specializing in alcohol abuse. More generally but equally relevant, managers should consider carefully whether they are dealing with *work-related* or purely private problems. If a manager decides he is not competent enough to deal with the problem, or that there is no relation to the work situation, he will have to use the skill of *situation clarification* (p. 28) and refer the employee.

Dealing with reactions to advice

When giving advice, the manager should pay close attention to the employee's reaction. After giving advice the manager should once again become a careful listener. Sometimes an employee may have doubts about the feasibility of the advice, or may feel a strong resistance to it. The manager can respond to such reactions by paraphrasing content or reflection of feelings (see p. 17). Thus the employee knows he is being taken seriously and the resistance may even diminish. Responses of this kind are certainly better than insisting on the advice being given. In relation to this we would like to mention the formula: $E = Q \times A$ (Vrolijk, 1991). Here

E stands for *Effect*, *Q* for *Quality* and *A* for *Acceptance*. In other words: the *E*ffect of advice does not just depend on its *Q*uality, but also on the *A*cceptance. No matter how sound the advice, if the employee does not accept it, the effect is zero. The formula also leads to the conclusion that the effect will be maximal if the quality of the advice is sound and the employee accepts it and acts on it. Of course an employee has the right to ignore any advice. If he does accept it, it is important to try and make *concrete agreements*. In another conversation the manager and employee can decide whether the advice has been beneficial (see also step 7, Evaluation of the general strategy). Figure 8.1 presents an overview of the personal problems interview.

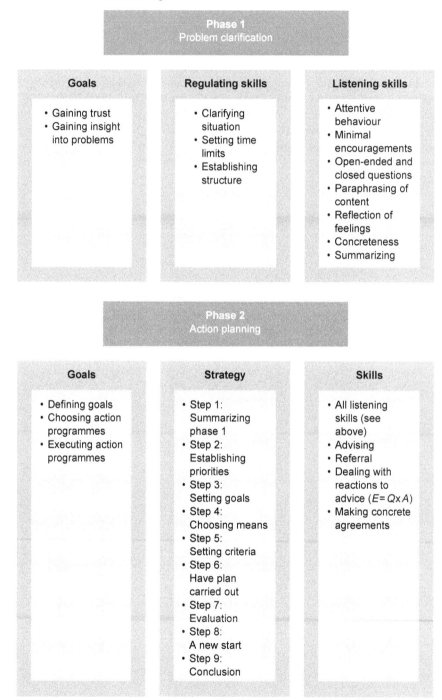

Figure 8.1 Overview of the personal problems interview

9   Handling complaints

Practical example

One of Dinner Ltd's clients is Bookdistri. Dinner Ltd has organized the dinner for Bookdistri's New Year party. Two days after the party, Paul Paper, the General Manager of Bookdistri, called Harry Haddock to say that he wanted to make an appointment for a meeting. After setting a date for the meeting, Harry asked whether Paul was satisfied about the party. Harry said that he had checked in on it around 10 pm and it seemed to him that people were having a wonderful time. Paul answered that that was precisely the reason he wished to speak to Harry, because there had been some problems later on in the evening. Because Paul Paper sounded a little irritated on the phone, Harry anticipates some difficulties will arise during their meeting. Usually clients have few or no complaints, or if they do they never tell him. Since Bookdistri is considered an important client that Dinner Ltd does not want to lose, Harry prepares well for the meeting.

Introduction

In daily work situations you will come across many situations involving people who have a complaint. The way you deal with these complaints determines whether guests or clients are lost forever or whether the relationship with them becomes stronger. Complaints from guests or clients may turn out to be a good point of departure for strengthening the relationship. Several studies have shown that clients will remain loyal to a company if it takes their complaints seriously and handles them well. However, this requires an attitude of believing that all complaints have a positive side and it also asks for active listening. Handling complaints consists of five phases:

1   Listening to the complaint.
2   Showing understanding.
3   Investigating the practical aspects of the complaint.

4   Finding a solution.
5   Coming to an agreement.

Listening to the complaint

If guests come to you with a complaint, they want only one thing: that you really listen to them, that you take the time for them and allow them to make their complaints. It is up to you to create an ideal situation and stimulate the guests to tell you their story. This calls for active listening. This phase determines whether your company will lose these guests forever or whether they will return on a regular basis.

Some of the listening skills you need to use in this phase are opening the conversation, attentive behaviour and the selective skills of paraphrasing and concreteness:

> After seating Paul Paper and offering him a cup of coffee, Harry Haddock comes straight to the point and opens the conversation by referring to their telephone call:

HARRY HADDOCK: On the phone you sounded somewhat irritated when I asked you about the New Year's party and you told me that was the reason you wanted to have this meeting.

PAUL PAPER: Yes, you've got that right. I really expected you guys to offer us something better than this. You've organized our New Year parties before and we never had any complaints. Maybe someone else was in charge this time because it really was a mess.

HARRY: I'm very sorry to hear this. Can you tell me what went wrong? [concreteness]

PAUL: Well, to begin with, there weren't enough plates. As you know we agreed that guests could take a new plate when they went to the buffet for a second time. But everybody had to use the same plate again. I asked your assistant to fix it, which he did immediately, but it was too late. You cannot expect people to use a plate to put a salad on after using it for a fish dish. And there wasn't enough white wine. Red was okay, so was beer and soda, but most people ate fish and they wanted to drink white wine with it.

Showing understanding

By reflection of feelings, for example, by saying 'Yes, I can see that must have really upset you' or 'You must be really disappointed', you indicate that you understand and respect the seriousness of the complaint. You then summarize the client's story to make sure you have understood it correctly.

Try to avoid justifying yourself or your company by explaining possible causes or making up reasons. Guests who have a complaint are not interested in possible causes; they want you to do something about the complaint.

HARRY: This situation must have been annoying for both the party guests and you. [reflection of feelings] Not only did we not supply enough plates so that guests could use clean ones whenever they wanted to eat something, but there wasn't enough white wine as well. As I understand it, Carl Campbell, my assistant, reacted quickly enough to your remark, but it didn't really matter anymore. [summary]

PAUL: Exactly.

HARRY: Was there anything else that you weren't happy about? [open question]

PAUL: No, this was it really, but it's important enough!

HARRY: Absolutely.

Investigating the practical aspects of a complaint

Sometimes a guest's story is clear but you don't have enough practical information to be able to solve the complaint. It may be necessary to know when an article has been bought, when the guest stayed in your hotel and in which room, when the guest had dinner in your restaurant and what they ate, the name of the guest and where they can be contacted. If you don't already know some or all of this information, now is the time to ask for it. The guest has had the chance to explain the complaint and will be open to finding possible solutions. Asking for details and practicalities will be interpreted as preparation for solving the problem:

HARRY: One thing I would like to know is: how many guests did attend the party?

PAUL: About 300 guests I would say.

Finding a solution

When you try to find a solution to a problem you must keep in mind that the solution has to satisfy the guest. No matter how well you have listened in the first phase, if you come up with a solution the guest doesn't like, you may give him the impression that the matter has not been taken seriously after all. A good way to find a suitable solution is to ask the guest to make a suggestion. Then together you can find out if the company can handle this and what the practical implications of the solution are.

When searching for a solution you must try to depart from the fact that the company is indeed responsible for the situation and that the complaint is an excellent opportunity to improve. Blaming the situation on the guest does not get you anywhere and will only lead to losing a customer. Ask open-ended questions to involve the guest in finding the solution:

HARRY: I would like to discuss some possible solutions to this problem with you to make sure things like this will not happen again. Would you have any ideas about how we could prevent this in the future?

PAUL: Well, it seemed to me that you somehow made a mistake when estimating the amounts. Maybe you should use a different number of plates and drinks per person. Or make sure you can get some very quickly. I didn't mind that your assistant Campbell went to get them, it just took too long. And there should have been enough wine.

HARRY: Yes, I was thinking along the same lines. I suggest we supply double the number of plates next time, and the same concerning the wine. In the meantime I'm thinking about a way to compensate you a little for the inconvenience.

PAUL: To be honest with you, I came here to get part of our money back. But that would be too much compensation, since we did have a nice party, and most people enjoyed themselves. Maybe you should refund some of it?

HARRY: That would be one possible solution. How about us offering you champagne at the next party?

PAUL: Okay, that would be fair compensation.

Sometimes, you may be involved in a situation where you only partly agree with the complaint. Another possibility is that you consider the complaint to be unreasonable. In both cases you are in a negotiation situation (see Chapter 15). The skill to be used then is 'reacting to criticism' (see p. 30). It is essential to make clear which part of the complaint you agree with and which part you do not. If the other party negotiates with you in a reasonable manner, you still can reach a solution that is acceptable for both parties.

Coming to an agreement

When you have found a solution that is acceptable for both parties, you must agree on how the solution will be implemented, who will take care of it and when:

HARRY: So we have decided that from now on we will double the number of plates per guest and do the same with the wine. As compensation Dinner Ltd will offer you champagne for the next party. I will confirm these agreements in a letter, which I will send you this week. I'll add the adjustments to your file. Let me know if you haven't received my letter by Friday. Thank you for coming to talk to me about this. Of course we want you to have a perfect party. Things like these should be avoided in the future.

Handling complaints in this way, by seeing complaints as a means to improve your company instead of an unpleasant event which needs to be dealt with quickly, will ensure a good relationship with guests or clients. Moreover, you may even attract more guests by word-of-mouth advertising thanks to the one with the complaint. (See Figure 9.1 for an overview of how to handle complaints.)

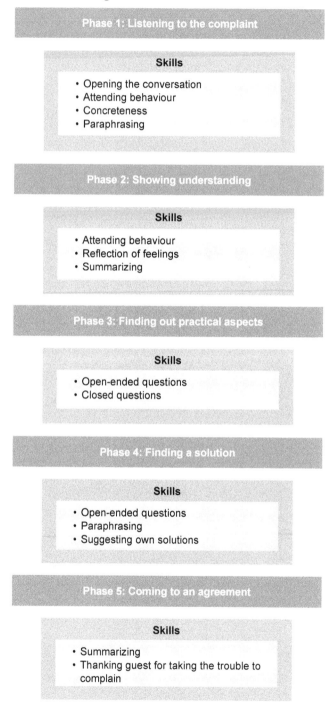

Figure 9.1 Overview of handling complaints

10   Breaking bad news

Practical example

Now that Carl Campbell, the Assistant F&B Manager, has found another job, headwaiter Ronald Rosenthal sees his chance. He has already been headwaiter for six years and he has always been able to see from close by how Carl organized his tasks. That is why he is pretty sure that the choice of a successor for Carl is little more than a formality. He will of course immediately be taken into consideration. Meanwhile, surely the directors and F&B Manager are convinced of his capabilities.

In reality it is not quite as he thinks. Director Freddy Fortune and F&B Manager Harry Haddock have already learned from Carl that Ronald wants to come in soon to talk about his successor. Ronald himself has even made a couple of remarks to Harry Haddock on several occasions which show that he thinks he has a good chance of succeeding Carl. But although Freddy and Harry find that Ronald does an excellent job as head waiter, they have come to the conclusion that he does not have the capabilities to fulfil the position of Assistant F&B Manager. It is true that he has enough experience in giving leadership to a team of temporary waiters, but they are afraid that he has too little insight to give adequate leadership when undertaking various big commissions. Also, in their opinion, he has too little experience in negotiating. Large amounts of money are usually involved and they consider it too big a risk to the organization if an inexperienced person conducts the negotiations.

Their decision has been made because of these reasons. An external application process is to be started. However, it is also necessary to tell Ronald the truth as soon as possible. The longer he lives with the illusion that he will succeed Carl, the greater the disappointment will be when eventually he sees that this is not to be the case. They arrange that Harry Haddock should invite Ronald for a conversation and tell him that in this case there is no chance of promotion to a higher position. Harry realizes that this is bad news for Ronald.

Introduction

In the practical example above, Harry Haddock is confronted with the tricky situation where he must deliver bad news. We give a number of other examples:

- The mentor of a trainee in the company must inform the trainee that he is to get a negative grading.
- A leader must tell a staff member that his temporary job will not be made permanent.
- The chairman of an application committee must tell a number of applicants that they will not be considered for the job for which they applied.
- The director must tell a head of department that his department is to be reorganized and cutbacks must be made.
- Due to poor achievements a boss must fire a staff member.

The goal of this chapter is to answer the question of how one should best deliver bad news. In the next section we make a distinction between the situation where one knows in advance that one has to deliver bad news, and the situation where this only becomes apparent during the conversation. We present a *conversation model for breaking bad news*. This model has three phases (Vrolijk, 1991): phase 1 – *delivering bad news immediately*; phase 2 – *how to deal with reactions*; phase 3 – *looking for solutions*. For each phase we first discuss the communication skills for the deliverer of the bad news. Then we handle a number of common 'inadequate' ways of reacting. For clarity's sake we refer to these as 'mistakes'. We close this chapter with a *summary* of the conversation model.

Two situations

In general, there are two types of bad news situations:

1   Situations in which one knows *immediately at the beginning of the conversation* that one has to deliver bad news.
2   Situations in which one realizes *during the conversation* that one has to break bad news.

An important point of difference is that in the first situation one can better *prepare* oneself than in the second situation, and can therefore turn up with more self-confidence. During preparation the deliverer of the bad news can anticipate *how* he wishes to conduct the conversation. He can also *think* about the formulation of the arguments. As far as this is concerned, two sorts of 'mistakes' can be made. Either the preparation of the argument is omitted ('We shall see how the conversation goes') or *too many* arguments are brought up. Ignoring the preparation phase leads to the situation where arguments have to be thought up during the conversation. This increases the chance that the deliverer of the news becomes emotionally involved. Badly formulated or weak arguments lead to putting the deliverer of bad news on the defensive. The disadvantage of too many arguments is that one often does not think about their strengths and weaknesses. It is incorrect to assume that people can be be persuaded by a large number of arguments. For example, it is better to present two strong arguments rather than five of varying degrees of strength, because the listener will almost certainly start debating the weaker ones.

If it only becomes apparent *during the conversation* that one must deliver bad news, for example, when a member of staff makes a request that the boss does not wish to grant, then one cannot prepare oneself in advance. Should the subject being tackled definitely involve bad news, then this should also be clearly indicated. If one is unsure, then it is better to play for time and to mention that you will look into that possibility. Although these two initial situations differ in their preparation time, in both the following *conversation model* can be applied.

Phase 1: Delivering bad news immediately

It is best to deliver bad news quickly. However, a short announcement may help to prepare the receiver of the bad news: for example, 'I am afraid that I have an unpleasant message for you.' Without such an announcement the bad news would really take the recipient by surprise. After that, you need to deliver the bad news immediately. Here it is important that you express the bad news calmly and clearly and show understanding for the difficult situation in which the other finds himself. It is advisable to restrict yourself to a *short explanation* at this phase: for example, 'I have to tell you that the temporary engagement will not be rearranged into a permanent one, because we are of the opinion that you do not satisfy in all regards the criteria for the position.' Afterwards the deliverer of the bad news should best remain *quiet* in order to give the other a chance to have an initial reaction.

Mistakes in phase 1

When the deliverer of bad news does not really know what to do with the situation, perhaps because he or she has not prepared for it properly, has not been granted the opportunity to do so, or has never been confronted with it before, then all kinds of 'mistakes' can be made. The background to these 'mistakes' is that the deliverer is not actually prepared to take responsibility for the delivery of bad news.

Putting it off

Sometimes people have a tendency to *put off* giving bad news. Then they talk about generalities, like the weather, or about the progress of a number of projects. You could say that this is a case of *avoidance reaction*, which is based on the fear of the other person's emotional reactions. The reality is that it becomes more and more difficult to come out with the bad news. It is highly probable that having finally heard the bad news the other party will react aggressively: 'First everything's sunny, and now you tell me this?'

The hang yourself method

With this method the deliverer tries to let the other discover the bad news himself. He can do this by asking suggestive questions: 'I suggest you must have seen for yourself that your department's figures for this last year are not what we expected.' When using this 'tactic', two reactions are conceivable. The first is that the other party does indeed 'tie the rope around his own neck'. In this case it seems that the tactic worked. Yet often after such a conversation the other is left with a sour taste in his mouth. The second possibility is that the other party will feel forced to draw negative conclusions and will often, if not openly, react with aggression: 'Aha, now I get it, you want to make cutbacks in our department. Now you tell me!'

Telling the news unclearly

The deliverer of the bad news may waffle vaguely: 'Yeah, uh, we have thought about this question long and hard and . . . uh . . . we have really looked at it from all angles . . . but uh . . . In truth your plan has little chance of succeeding.' All this beating about the bush is highly likely to irritate the other person.

Giving detailed arguments

Giving *an overly long explanation* in the first phase of the conversation is not useful. This is due to the fact that the other has just heard the bad news and is too emotional for a long explanation. Usually only a small fraction of the conversation is retained because of the numbed reaction that often follows the reception of bad news.

Phase 2: How to deal with reactions

As previously mentioned, the other party will in the first instance often react emotionally to the bad news. The differences in emotional reactions between people can vary greatly. One person may stare at you fixedly, turn pale and stay quiet; another may immediately react strongly and threaten to appeal against the decision. Below is a summary of the most common emotions and behaviours.

1   *Shock.* When bad news comes unexpectedly, the recipient often reacts first with shock and confusion. 'What? How is that possible!?' Sometimes people are literally struck dumb and do not know how they should react.
2   *Aggression.* As a consequence of the frustration that the bad news brings about, the other may become angry. This anger can take the form of light irritation and curt reactions, but can also manifest as open rage.
3   *Disbelief.* The other person may ask questions like: 'How is it possible? I have done my very best to finish off the project within the set deadlines, haven't I?'
4   *Arousing the sympathy of the deliverer.* Some people can consciously or subconsciously take such a position that the deliverer of the bad news starts to feel guilty. These people do not kick up a fuss, but portray themselves as meek and sorrowful.
5   *Perseverance.* This means that people constantly react in the same way, like a broken record player: 'Oh, how that disappoints me . . . Yes, that really does disappoint me' and so on.

The goal of the deliverer of bad news in this second phase is to give the other person the opportunity to react and to deal with the *emotional reactions* as well as possible. First, the deliverer must listen attentively to the reactions. Second, he can 'deal with the emotional reaction' by expressing understanding and remaining calm and serious. To express understanding one can make use of such conversational skills as *paraphrasing of content* and *reflection of feeling* (see p. 17). Especially with bad news, where the emotional reactions can be very strong, it is important to use an appropriate intensity of expression when reflecting feelings:

HEADWAITER RONALD ROSENTHAL: If you do not revoke your decision, I'm going to the director!
HARRY: I understand that you are livid and are willing to do anything to undo the decision. [*not: I see that you are a little bit angry*]

When the other person really does not want to accept the bad news yet, it is advisable to repeat it from time to time in a businesslike tone.

As mentioned, the recipient can also react with aggression. The aggression can be directed at the *information that* is conveyed, at the deliverer himself, or at the whole organization. If the aggression directs itself at the deliverer, then it is a case of *identifying* the bad news with the deliverer. (The classic example of this was the messenger who informed the emperor

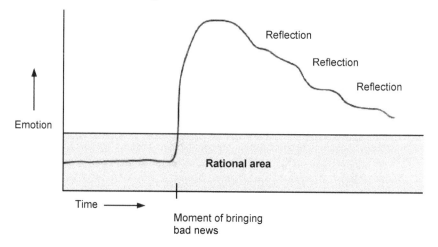

Figure 10.1 Influence of reflections of feeling on information processing

of a lost battle: the messenger was decapitated.) The aggression that is directed at the deliverer personally is always difficult to accept. First, there is often nothing that can be done if the decision is badly received. Second, the deliverer would also prefer to be giving good news. Third, the deliverer is trying to present the bad news with understanding, yet still the other person is getting angry! In such a situation it can be sensible to realize that the other does not usually mean it personally. Aggression is after all a common reaction to frustration and the other person must do something with their reaction in the moment. When the deliverer fully realizes this in advance, he will be more successful in dealing with such aggression with a measure of calm and understanding. This is part of working professionally.

The duration of the second phase is dependent on the gravity of the bad news and the personal reaction of the other. Only when the first emotions have abated somewhat is the other party ready to hear further arguments and perhaps to think of alternative solutions to the problem in question. Voorendonk (1986) sketches the link between emotional and rational information processing (see Figure 10.1).

In Figure 10.1, emotion is depicted as a function of time. Immediately after delivering the bad news we see a steep climb of the emotional level to far above the (symbolic) 'rational area'. This means that the rational thinking faculty of the other is temporarily impaired. Through showing understanding for the emotions one can tone them down somewhat, which slowly increases the possibility for rational information processing. The other person begins to see the facts more clearly and often becomes more receptive to an extended explanation of the bad news. They may demonstrate being ready for further discussion: 'But explain to me why the decision has been taken' or 'What should I do now?'

At this stage the deliverer should have the arguments clearly lined up. He can then explain them one by one. After each argument it is important to give the other the opportunity to react. There is always a chance that the other party may still react emotionally to an argument. In dealing with reactions to each argument, 'paraphrasing of content' and 'reflection of feelings' are again applicable skills, as is the giving of any subsequent clear information.

Mistakes in phase 2

However logical the above may sound, it is highly probable that the deliverer allows himself to be led into giving a personal reaction, which is perhaps understandable in daily life. Then one can react very directly and personally, but as a professional one should try to avoid this. Here follow a number of common 'wrong' reactions:

1   *Reacting with contra-aggression.* Instead of remaining calm if the other becomes angry or irritated, the deliverer also reacts with aggressive comments. The consequence of such actions is that the conversation loses its businesslike nature and threatens to escalate into argument.
2   *Extensive defence.* Anyone who goes on to defend the negative decision extensively often feels personally guilty. This is not businesslike either. It is best to limit the arguments to two or three important ones. Presenting too many arguments can result in getting lost in fruitless discussion.
3   *Sugaring the pill.* By sugaring the pill we mean presenting the bad news in such a way that it almost becomes good news: for example, by pointing out that there are all sorts of advantages attached to the bad news. There are of course people who may allow themselves to be 'taken in' if someone sugars the pill. However, it is more likely that they will later see that the situation has been more attractively presented than reality allows, with the possible consequence of delayed aggressive reactions (another conversation, a letter). Whatever the case, it is fairer to deliver the bad news as it is and not to dress it up.
4   *Playing it down.* By 'playing it down' we mean presenting bad news as something insignificant, something that does not need to be taken seriously. The consequence of playing down reactions is that the other does not feel the extent of his first reactions has been fully understood. Because of this, emotions can escalate: the more you soothe, the stronger the other will react.
5   *It's no fun for me either!* Instead of getting involved in the feelings of the other, the deliverer directs attention to his own difficult position: for example, 'Yes, you must believe that I find the whole thing most disagreeable. You are the third person I have had to disappoint this week [sigh]. But well, it's just the way it goes.'

Phase 3: Looking for solutions

In the preceding paragraphs we have pointed out that one should only look for solutions when the bad news has been somewhat absorbed. Whether the other person is ready can often be deduced from comments such as: 'But what should we do then?' Sometimes such a question fails to arise and then one must carefully move on to this phase: for example, 'I understand that this must disappoint you terribly. Shall we try, though, to see if there are other possibilities to do something?' In this example the deliverer of the bad news explicitly introduces the phase of looking for solutions. Then one can best allow the other to speak about possible solutions. For if the deliverer starts in with alternatives, a reasonable chance exists that the other may reject them out of frustration. Only when the other has given their own possible solution may the deliverer come up with any other information about possible solutions. It is not advisable to be too optimistic about this phase. Often bad news is simply bad news and there are no simple solutions. In this case there is no alternative but for both parties to accept the situation, however difficult that might be for them: 'I'm sorry, but I really can't help you with this problem.' Such a reaction may appear hard, but it is often more honest than feverishly to seek solutions that do not have a chance of success anyway. To *round off* the conversation one can *summarize* what was decided during the conversation. One can declare oneself prepared to answer any questions that may arise later.

Mistakes in phase 3

When someone has delivered bad news they may often find it unfortunate for the other and like nothing more than to make it a little better, so they look for solutions. This can result in allowing the other too little time to absorb their emotions. Common 'mistakes' in phase 3 include:

1   *Starting phase 3 too soon.* One can proceed to the third phase too fast. For example, the other may already ask: 'What now?' at the beginning of phase 2, but in fact be still too emotional to think about it rationally.
2   *Zealously thinking of solutions yourself.* The more solutions coming from the deliverer, the greater the risk that the solutions are not applicable to the circumstances of the other. The intentions may be very good, but the chances are that the latter will criticize or reject such solutions.

Figure 10.2 presents an overview of how to break bad news.

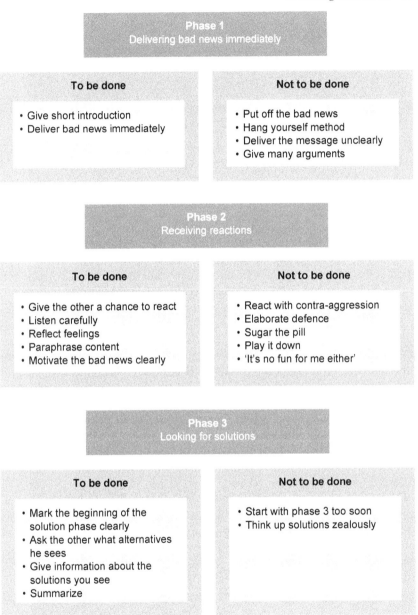

Figure 10.2 Overview of breaking bad news

11 The sales interview

Practical example

The Thames Hotel in London has been renovated and is going to give a big reception for its reopening. Although the kitchen and restaurant staff of the Thames Hotel will take care of part of the catering themselves, they will need catering assistance to make the reception a success. The Thames Hotel has asked three catering companies to come up with a proposal. Dinner Ltd is one of the selected companies and is very interested in catering for this reception. In general, these types of assignments are a challenge to the company. Catering for a prestigious hotel like the Thames Hotel is very good for the reputation of Dinner Ltd and both the headwaiters and temporary waiters welcome the opportunity to show their professionalism.

Gerald Glass (Commercial Director) has taken the Thames Hotel assignment to Harry Haddock (F&B Manager) and Jenny Jacobson (Finance and Administration) with the request to make a proposal. After three weeks the first tender is ready and Gerald, Harry and Jenny go over the figures to see how their plan can be clarified and defended during the interview Gerald will have with the representatives of the Thames Hotel.

Gerald has set it as his goal to get this assignment. He will have to be well prepared and to have carefully considered the situation in order to beat his colleagues from the other catering companies. These companies could of course also do excellent work and be interested in the assignment for the same reasons.

Why should the Thames Hotel choose Dinner Ltd? First, because Dinner Ltd probably delivers the same quality work as the other companies, but at a lower price. Second, maybe because some of the temporary workers have worked for the Thames Hotel before, or because they have thought of more creative dishes than the two other companies. Gerald and Harry consider the quality of their product, in this case catering for prestigious hotels. Furthermore they put together a list of possible requests and demands that are not yet incorporated into the design that the Thames Hotel will probably come up with during the interview. In this way they are trying to find common ground between the demands of Thames Hotel and what

Dinner Ltd can offer. They try to present their ideas with hopefully decisive arguments.

The interview is held on the date set and a well-briefed Gerald Glass goes to the Thames Hotel. He is full of ideas in order to get the assignment, but at the same time he feels a bit nervous because he doesn't know what his rivals will be presenting.

Introduction

The sales interview has a very obvious goal. The seller (sender) wants to sell his product to a buyer (receiver). There cannot be any misunderstanding about this and both parties know it. The road to that goal is however much less obvious and contains many hurdles, one of which is the seller's technique.

In general we can distinguish two selling techniques: the situation in which the customer contacts the salesperson; the situation in which the salesperson goes out and looks for potential clients for the product or service. In the first situation, customers have already completed a large part of the process that leads to the purchasing of the product. They have already decided that they want to be informed about the product and they know more or less what the seller is offering. In the second situation, customers have to start the decision process from the beginning. Although the sales interview in both situations consists of the same successive phases, the execution of these phases will sometimes differ.

In this chapter we discuss the preparation of the sales interview, the structure of the sales interview, and the interviewing skills that are important at each phase. Finally, we summarize with an overview of the different phases together with the relevant skills involved.

Preparation

A thorough preparation of a sales interview is half the work. First, sellers should try to find out the needs and wants of the customer. Second, they should have in mind a list of the qualities of the product or service. They should ask themselves which qualities of their product fit well with the wishes and needs of the client. If sellers are able to make a relationship between these two areas, they can provide some strong arguments to promote their product:

> Gerald Glass can, for example, link the experience of the company with prestigious hotels as a special quality fitting the needs of the Thames Hotel. The fact that one of their headwaiters and a couple of temporary waiters have worked for the Thames Hotel in the past means that Dinner Ltd can adapt quickly to the organizational culture of the Thames Hotel.

During the preparation stage, sellers should also think about the structure of the sales interview. They have to decide what they want to bring up at each phase of the interview, and when they want to give room to the customers. Finally salespersons should prepare themselves for any possible objections that customers may bring up and the way they will react to them. We now discuss the structure of this interview.

Structure

In a sales interview we can distinguish three phases: the orientation phase, the central phase and the decision-making phase. In some instances, the sale may take place after several interviews. The different phases of the selling process then require different interviews. In some selling situations the end of the interview coincides with the closing off of one of the phases. In other situations salespersons need to pick up a phase that has not been completed at the next interview.

During the orientation phase the seller and customers become acquainted with each other. The goal and time are decided upon and information is exchanged. During this phase salespersons should try to get a good idea of the customer's wishes and raise their interest in the product or service.

In the central phase arguing is the most important skill. Here salespersons can profit from their preparations and link the qualities of their product or service with the needs of the customer. They should deal with customer's wishes in order of importance. They can also try to resolve any objections customers might have and turn them into solvable problems. During this phase, the so-called negotiations take place about the solutions (product/service) that the salespersons suggest for the customer's needs.

Finally, the decision phase consists of an elaboration of the decision that has been reached at the end of the central phase. This can mean that customers will accept the proposal. It is also possible that they want more information before they come to a definite decision or that they do not accept the proposal. We deal with the different phases successively in the sections below.

Orientation phase

In situations in which salespersons go out themselves to visit potential customers, the first phase begins with the mutual or renewed acquaintance. The salespersons state the goal of their visit and ask how much time customers have available for the interview. Ideally customers will determine the duration of the conversation. In order to avoid misunderstandings, we note here that the goal of the interview can be the introduction of a new product, or in response to a request to be further informed or the 'keeping open' of previous contacts. If the appointment has been made in advance, salespersons should mention the time that the customers have taken for this interview. Customers then know what they can expect and are more readily willing to spend the agreed time on the interview than if they are overwhelmed and find each minute they spend too long, because they were actually doing something else. In situations in which customers visit salespersons they will often indicate their goal and usually no agreements are made regarding the duration of the interview.

After the opening sentences it is necessary for salespersons to acquire a good understanding of the customer's needs. This can be achieved by paraphrasing the customer's needs and making them concrete. By asking openended questions, salespersons can make a priority list of the customer's wishes:

> The interview of Gerald Glass by the Thames Hotel could show that providing appropriate dishes and drinks for guests from various countries is the number one priority.

When salespersons have acquired a good understanding of the needs of customers, they can summarize what has been discussed and ask whether the customer agrees. It is important that customers feel their wishes are taken seriously and that salespersons are helping to find solutions. When customer's requirements have been clarified, salespersons should try to raise interest in their product or service. They may do this with a few well-prepared sentences from which it is clear that their product or service links up very well with the wishes and needs of the customer. For example, in an interview with the municipal building committee Gerald Glass says:

> 'Gentlemen. I believe that Dinner Ltd has come up with some good solutions for some of the problems regarding vegetarian and Islamic guests. This will interest you, Mr. Olivetti, as you do business with so many guests from Islamic countries.' Gerald gives an inviting look to the PR Manager in the hope that he will feel involved, first, because he is known to do business with people from Islamic countries, and second because vegetarian and Islamic guests are provided for in Dinner Ltd's plan.

During this confronting part of the interview it is important that salespersons can actually show something. Using presentation folders with pictures or drawings they can try to give an accurate image of what they have to offer:

> For this purpose Dinner Ltd has brought menus, recipes and photographs. Gerald Glass also has a presentation folder in which he can show the menus that they have used for catering projects similar to the Thames Hotel assignment.

Central phase

The interests of customers that have been raised in the orientation phase now need to be strongly supported. At this stage salespersons can make use of their prepared arguments. They should show that a number of the customer's needs and wishes could be fulfilled.

The requirements of the Thames Hotel may be: first, it wants to cater for 1000 guests at £25 per head; second, it wants the hot dishes prepared in its own kitchens; third, the reception should appear to be completely catered for by Thames Hotel itself. Gerald Glass can then argue as follows:

> As you can see we can offer a good variety of dishes and beverages for the price per guest. The combination of hot and cold dishes is such that all hot dishes can be prepared in the Thames Hotel kitchen. And finally, we can rent uniforms so all waiters will wear the same dress.

Very often customers will have objections and salespersons would do well to anticipate some of them in advance and think of answers, keeping to the following order: *buying arguments – objections – counterarguments*. By starting with the buying arguments they can already solve some of the customer's objections. Moreover, in the case of an unexpected objection, they gain time to think about their answer to it. Of course they will need to announce that they would like to rediscuss objections at a later stage.

When the arsenal of arguments, objections and counterarguments has been depleted, the decision-making phase has arrived. Sometimes the arguments will be repeated because the customer is still hesitating. Sometimes the customer may be convinced of the quality of the offered product or service and decide immediately. Unfortunately, it also sometimes happens that the customer is not satisfied and prefers to deal with another company – but that is the life of a salesperson.

Decision-making phase

In some selling situations customers will take the initiative to move on to the decision-making phase. The salespersons can also initiate the decision phase themselves by giving a summary of what has been discussed so far. At this stage they will be hoping to hear the customer's decision and trying to find out whether they are willing to buy or not. Often a small sentence such as 'What do you think?' will be necessary to get an answer.

If customers keep hesitating salespersons can make use of an ending technique. Korswagen (1987) mentions the isolation technique and advantages–disadvantages reasoning. We emphasize that both techniques should be used to get clarity and not to manipulate the customer.

The *isolation technique* is a way to reduce the customer's hesitations to some concrete points. Customers may sometimes be confused by the sheer volume of information. A clear ordering may give them a better view of the arguments in favour or against the purchase. Salespersons summarize the points that the customers agree with and ask for their approval. Then they mention the points causing hesitation and also ask for approval. The customer's hesitancy can therefore be reduced to one or two issues that can sometimes be clearly put aside by the salespersons.

In *advantages–disadvantages reasoning*, salespersons take the initiative clearly to compare the advantages with the disadvantages. They write the arguments for buying or accepting the offer below each other on a piece of paper and ask the customer to write the counterarguments next to them. Salespersons can now focus on the counterarguments that remain.

The end of the sales interview is drawing close. There are three ways in which the interview can be ended:

- the customer decides not to accept the offer
- the customer wants more time, extra information or another interview
- the customer accepts the offer or gives the assignment.

In the first case, if despite all their efforts salespersons have not achieved any direct results, it is important that they part from the customer on good terms. The relationship needs to be continued. Maybe they might be able to offer each other something at a later stage. Both are representatives of the organizations for which they work. The image of the organization that has been presented can only be positive if the unsuccessful meetings end in mutual respect. In concrete terms this means that salespersons need to comprehend the arguments of customers who don't want to buy or give the assignment. Respect should be evident in both welcoming and departing conversations.

If customers haven't yet made a decision, salespersons should make sure that they keep the communication channels open. They should arrange to send any missing information as soon as possible, suggest another visit or push for another interview and immediately try to make an appointment.

In the third (ideal) case, when customers decide to buy the product or to give the assignment, only the issue of correct business handling, formalities and saying thank you remain. Salespersons should take leave of customers by thanking them for the pleasant interaction and expressing their hopes and expectations that customers will thoroughly enjoy the delivered product or service.

Communication skills

The description of these three stages shows that salespersons need to have both a flexible and tenacious attitude in relation to their customers. This attitude means that they should give in at times ('I agree. How would you like to solve that?') in order to come back at the right moment with their proposition ('You mention that as a possible solution, but what if we take a look at the way we can transform my proposal to that extent?'). In order to be able to show a respectful attitude, salespersons need to make use of the skills mentioned in Part I. We now discuss the most important communication skills required for each selling phase.

In order to find out what the customer's needs and wishes are, the emphasis during the *orientation phase* is on the correct use of listening skills. If they want to explore such needs and wishes, salespersons will have to ask open-ended questions. If they want more precise information or more concrete facts, they will have to request a specification at the right moment and ask closed questions. Salespersons need to give the customers the feeling that they are truly interested in their motives and should stimulate them, by using attentive behaviour, by paraphrasing and by reflection of feelings. If salespersons feel that they have been adequately informed about the wishes of the customers, they can summarize what has been discussed. They should do so tentatively, so that customers get a chance to correct them if necessary.

Salespersons should also use some regulating skills in order to maintain the structure of the interview. When presenting their product or service, they need to use their assertive skills. Salespersons should present information about their product or service in a clear and structured way.

The *central phase* consists of the dialogue between salespersons and customers. In this phase the salesperson should link the qualities of their product or service to the needs and wishes of the customer. A good, attractive and succinct formulation is now very important. By using words such as 'cost efficient' and 'economical' they can emphasize the financial advantages of their proposal. With words such as 'special', 'different' and 'remarkable' they are emphasizing its exclusiveness. Of course salespersons will try to use words that are in line with the needs of their customers.

When listening to the objections of customers, salespersons should use the listening skills which they have also applied in the first phase to ascertain customer needs, and the sender skill 'reacting to criticism' (see p. 30). Customers should get the feeling that they are being informed in a professional manner and should not have the idea that they are being 'talked into something'.

During the *decision phase* salespersons should try to end the interview in a positive manner. Here they can make use of regulating skills. They should keep an eye on the time that customers have available, use silences to give them the opportunity to think quietly about it, clarify the situation if necessary, not ask new questions and try to bring the conversation to a successful closure. The interview is now ended. If it turns out that the customers still has some misgivings, it is better to make an appointment for another meeting.

Figure 11.1 presents an overview of the sales interview.

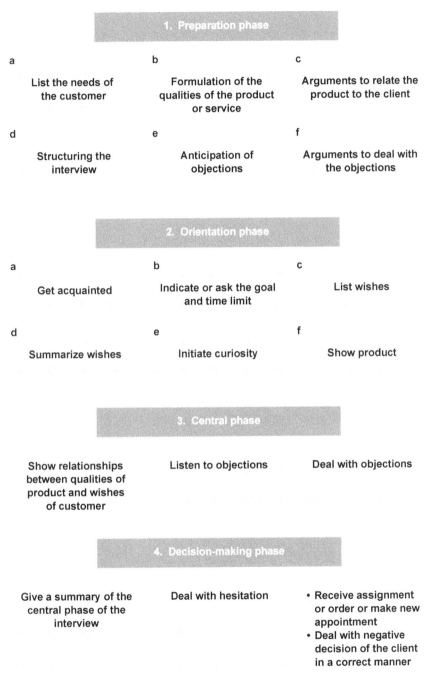

Figure 11.1 Overview of the sales interview

Part III

Group conversations

Introduction

In Part III we deal with various kinds of conversations in organizations that are held by more than two people: conversations where decisions must be made, measures must be taken, or where policies must be defined. Conversations where more than two people take part demand a diversity of skills. Apart from basic communication skills such as active listening behaviour and the ability to formulate one's own ideas, opinions and interpretations, group conversations demand regulating skills: the bringing about and maintenance of a conversational structure. Above all, knowledge and insight into decision making, problem solving and strategy development are vital.

Group conversations are more complex then dialogues: there are more senders and more receivers. Therefore misunderstandings arise more quickly. A skilful conversation leader can bring about a worthwhile contribution to the efficacy of group discussion. By 'efficacy' we mean that the goal striven for by the conversation is achieved. In Chapter 12 we present an example of a method to reach a decision with the participation of all group members, a so-called phase model. This decision-making method forms the thread running through the various forms of meeting that are discussed in Chapter 12. In Chapter 13 we discuss a model and the communication skills for leading meetings. Differences of opinion can lead to conflict. Conflict management is the subject of Chapter 14. A specific skill is negotiation. Just as within the organization itself as with external relations, employees change in situations where negotiation is necessary. We focus on this theme in Chapter 15. In Chapter 16 we describe a model and skills for giving presentations.

12 Decision making

Practical example

The staff association of Dinner Ltd is very active and plays an important role in giving shape to the culture of the organization. Its broadly shared mission is: 'Working together'. This means that the feeling of unity among staff members needs to be developed. The goal of the staff association is to further such unity in a variety of ways. However, the interests and priorities of the different staff members are varied. The programme of the yearly personnel day is often a source of much criticism. For some it is a successful day only if many sport activities are planned; for others the day cannot go wrong as long as there is plenty of liquid refreshment to hand. It takes quite a bit of head-breaking to make the programme varied enough to appease everyone. The committee of the staff association is composed of representatives from all layers of Dinner Ltd. Bert Berman is the chairman. He is not happy with the way the decisions are taken. The meetings run somewhat chaotically, with ideas flying back and forth across the table and being immediately taken on or criticized. This is combined with much bickering, personal observations and remarks. In Bert's opinion, reactions are given much too quickly before other alternatives have been thoroughly discussed. Bert wants decisions to be made in a different way.

Introduction

When important decisions have to be taken in an organization, a number of people are usually involved. The more people who take part in the decision-taking process, the more opinions, experience and knowledge are involved concerning the points to be decided. Therefore, there is a greater chance that a well-considered decision is reached than if only one person had been involved. Besides, more people are likely to be inclined to carry out the decision if they actually participated in the decision taking. They are aware of the arguments that led to the decision, they know which general alternatives were named and why these were rejected. In this way, it may appear that within an organization all decisions are best taken by all concerned.

However, there are considerable drawbacks associated with decision taking when a large number of people are involved. First, it takes a lot of time and input from all the participants. Not only does it demand preparedness and the skill to listen to other people's opinions, but also the willingness to give up one's own standpoint. Second, the danger exists that group decisions are made on the grounds of a one-sided viewpoint, because the participants have identical interpretations and strengthen one another's opinions. Then there are insufficient people represented holding different views. Third, there may be a possible deficiency of skills. If the necessary skills to lead the decision-taking process in the right direction are not present, then insufficient discussion of the various possibilities and the arguments can result. Again this can end with over-hasty or unsound decisions being made.

There are both advantages and disadvantages to a decision-taking process in which a number of participants are involved. Within an organization the balance of pros and cons must be made before embarking on a decision-taking process involving the participation of different parties. Vroom and Yetton (1973) describe a number of situations that are appropriate for this:

- the various parties have a need for a lot of information regarding the various aspects of the subject in question
- the nature of the question is unclear: what is it actually about, what is the problem, what are the causes and the consequences?
- a question of the employees is acknowledged as a problem
- employees consider the resolution of a problem or the handling of a problem important
- acceptance of the decision is relevant for its implementation
- employees feel the need for independence
- the time limit is not too pressing.

There are various ways of coming to a decision together. In this chapter we discuss a phase model, the goal of which is to reach a decision with the participation of various parties. Every phase has its pitfalls and we cover these phases one by one and illustrate them with the practical example of Dinner Ltd. We then deal with the difficulties that must be overcome at each phase and the communication skills required by discussion leaders. Three techniques to develop a group solution or strategy are described. The chapter ends with an overview of the decision-making process.

Phases in the decision-making process

In an organization countless decisions must be taken daily. For example, during a work consultation decisions must be taken regarding division of tasks in the carrying out of various projects. We do not concern ourselves here with this type of decision, but rather limit ourselves to situations where the taking of decisions is often the most difficult: namely situations that are viewed as undesirable and therefore demanding change.

Phase 0: Point out the undesirable (present) situation

If people within an organization believe that a current *situation* no longer fulfils certain criteria, this can be the beginning of a changing process and of the necessity of making decisions to bring about change. The situation gives rise to feelings of uneasiness and causes criticism. To bring about change the unsatisfied person must express their dissatisfaction with the existing situation and the willingness to do something about it must be present:

> At Dinner Ltd dissatisfaction prevails about the completion of the personnel day. There is often criticism about the programme, the decision taking does not run smoothly, some employees feel unappreciated and dumbfounded. What can be done?

Phase 1: Describe the current situation

The vaguely felt dissatisfaction with the situation must be made clearer. What is wrong exactly? What causes the dissatisfaction? Can facts be named which make the dissatisfaction concrete, or events that clarify the situation?

> At the next committee meeting of the staff association Bert Berman verbalizes his dissatisfaction about the situation. Do the others also hear such regular negative noises about the personnel day? From whom do these come? Are the others satisfied with the way in which the decision about the completion is taken? What is the reason that so few people are enthusiastic about the personnel day?

Phase 2: Describe the desired situation

When it is clear what is wrong about the present situation, it is possible to describe how the ideal or desirable situation should be. By describing the discrepancy between the problem situation and the desired situation, the problem can be formulated. The description of the desired situation includes an aim that can be striven for. The question is about what obstructions prevent reaching this goal:

> During the committee meeting it becomes clear that there are relatively few employees who participate with pleasure in the yearly personnel day. In an ideal situation most of the people should look back upon such a day with pleasure. People should get to know one another in a

different way than during the normal working hours. Such a personnel day should be an instrument towards furthering unity. Why doesn't it work like this?

Phase 3: Formulate problems and obstructions

When it has become clear what is lacking in the present situation and how the desired situation should be, it is possible to formulate the problem in clear wording. The removal of obstructions usually forms the key to the solution of the problem. At the same time, it is important during this phase to see the consequences of the undesirable situation. The severity of the problem can be deduced from the answer. A comparison can be made between the costs of the effort required to remove the obstructions and the profits that arise from the disappearance of the negative consequences:

Bert Berman formulates the problem of the personnel day at the end of phase 3 as follows: The personnel day does not achieve its aim of 'promoting unity amongst employees'. The result is the forming of subgroups and 'separation of spirits'. The obstructions that have been mentioned are:

- people do not feel involved
- the programme scarcely meets the wishes of a single group
- the day is too loosely structured
- the programme does not consist of any parts whereby people get to know one another.

Phase 4: Thinking of strategies

During this phase the whole group should be able to name all the possible strategies to remove the obstruction in order to reach the desired situation. By 'strategy' we mean a plan to tackle the problem. This is the most creative phase of the whole decision-taking process and it is important that no single value judgement is iterated about the strategies proposed. The more strategies that are thought up, the more chance that new and unusual ideas will be developed:

During the committee meeting of the staff association the following ideas are brought up: occupying an uninhabited island together; organizing a survival course; hiring two-man canoes and alternating the crews with people from all levels within Dinner Ltd; hiring barges without skippers; organizing a Mafia party; organizing a sixties party; organizing a step-in programme; a dinner dance in which partners, children and dogs participate; abandon the personnel day.

In the last part of this chapter we examine three methods which can be used during this phase.

Phase 5: Testing strategies on the basis of criteria

When all the ideas have been exhausted and all the strategies to reach the desired situation have been listed, with the help of a board or flipchart if necessary, then it can be investigated which strategies or possible combinations of strategies come into consideration for further development. At this stage criteria must be set by which strategies can be tested. The criteria must be such that the chosen strategies fulfil the aim. Moreover, a number of practical criteria can be named which the strategy should meet:

> Bert Berman has written all the mentioned strategies on a flipchart and named criteria which the strategies must fulfil:
>
> - feasibility: to what degree can the strategies practically be carried out?
> - profits: to what extent does the strategy contribute to the raising of the obstacles? Is the strategy effective?
> - costs: what are the strategy's costs, in time, money and energy?
> - do the costs balance against the profits?

Phase 6: The taking of a decision

Now the stage has been reached where a definite choice must be made. With the help of the criteria various strategies have been rejected and some selected. Sometimes it is possible to perform a number of ideas simultaneously:

> At Dinner Ltd the decision is eventually made to have a step-in programme, whereby employees can make a choice between one or more programme sections, depending on their interests and fitness: a trip wading in the mudflats, a canoe trip, a museum trip, a hooded cart trip. The day will be rounded off with a barbecue where representatives of the various groups will give an eye-witness account of their programme-section. A prize will be awarded for the most original contribution.

Phase 7: Division of tasks

When it has eventually been decided how the problem is to be solved, a discussion of the tasks is still needed:

- What tasks must be performed?
- How should this be done?
- Who will do what?
- When do the various tasks have to be completed?

The tasks will be carried out accordingly.

Phase 8: Evaluation of the consequences of the decision

After some time it will be discovered whether or not the chosen decision has indeed led to the desired situation. Adjustments may have to be made before everyone is satisfied with the result:

> After the personnel day of Dinner Ltd, which went according to the procedure agreed upon, Bert Berman (chairman) and Charlotte Cohen (secretary) compile a survey that they distribute amongst all employees. The survey consists of a number of questions regarding the most and least appreciated sections of the programme and asks for suggestions for improvement.

Pitfalls

Here we have described an ideal model. The phases are neatly completed, step by step, resulting in a decision with which all participants are satisfied. Unfortunately, in actual practice the process of decision taking, even with the help of a structured model such as described here, is often less satisfactory.

Each phase has its difficulties. It is the task of the group in general and the possible group leader in particular to perceive these difficulties and bring the conversation back to the aim. In phases 1 and 2, in which the *problem is not yet clearly formulated*, confusion often reigns regarding what the problem is, or what one supposes the problem to be. The problem is often confused with the symptoms. For example, is the dissatisfaction with the personnel day at Dinner Ltd the problem, or is it the day's programme? People often have a tendency to search quickly for an explanation of situations that they do not have under control. This can result in group members pointing out a scapegoat for the disagreeable situation. For example, the half-heartedness of the employees of Dinner Ltd could be pointed out to be the cause of all the dissatisfaction. With such an attitude the necessity of actively seeking solution strategies can be killed at an early stage.

Participants may start seeking solutions even before the problem is clear due to a tendency quickly to put an end to uncertain situations. The first thing that should happen in phase 3 is reaching *agreement on the definition of the problem.* Is the problem discussed so far the 'real' problem or is there another problem behind it?

> The staff association of Dinner Ltd can now try, for example, to improve staff unity by means of the personnel day, but if the real problem is 'friendship politics' or 'subgroup forming', then a new programme cannot solve the real problem.

For the conversation leader the listening skills 'asking questions', 'paraphrasing', 'reflection of feelings', 'concreteness' and 'summarizing' are important in order to outline the dissatisfaction with the present situation and to acquire a clear picture of the desired situation. The conversation leader closes phase 3 with a clear formulation, which is understood and agreed upon by all participants.

In phase 4, in which *strategies are developed*, there are a number of pitfalls. One of the most common is the immediate discussion of each strategy that has been mentioned. Appraisal and disapproval are immediately expressed, which is often obstructive for the creative process. The group then conforms too quickly. A second pitfall is that strategies put forward by people who enjoy a high status within the group receive disproportionate attention and value in relation to strategies introduced by people who are less respected. If a solution immediately prompts negative reactions, then the people who offered the strategy can quickly become discouraged. A third pitfall is grasping for solutions that have rendered a service in the past, without looking for new solutions.

An important communication skill for the conversation leader at this phase is 'attentive behaviour'. Eye contact, a warm, respectful attitude and intonation and use of 'minimal encouragers' stimulate participants to offer their contributions. By making a clear rejection of discussion, the conversation leader can hold the group to the agreement that during this stage ideas are collected and not yet evaluated. The conversation leader may use the skill 'situation clarification' to achieve this end.

During the *testing of strategies* in phase 5, the possibility exists that participants do not thoroughly think through the consequences of all strategies because they already have a definite preference. Another obstacle during this phase is the tendency for people to identify a strategy with the person who put it forward, meaning that the strategies can no longer be objectively compared. The conversation skills that the conversation leader should use frequently at this phase are 'asking questions', 'paraphrasing', 'concreteness' and 'summarizing'.

The *closing phase*, in which the decision is taken, has difficult moments of its own. One of the problems, the overvaluing of strategies contributed by important or likeable people, has already been mentioned. Another difficulty is getting the approval of all those present. Unjustly, silence is often interpreted as consent. During this phase conversation leaders will make especial use of the listening skills 'concreteness' and 'summarizing'. If they suspect that the silent people are not in consent, then in order to attain clarity they should voice this suspicion with a reflection of feeling: 'I see some people frowning. Are there any objections to the proposal?'

Here we have sketched a number of problems per phase, which the conversation leader can handle with the help of the communication skills covered in Part I. In this way his leadership should ensure that:

- all those present get the opportunity to offer their contributions
- all contributions receive attention
- all contributions are thoroughly thought through
- all contributions have an equal chance of selection.

Three techniques to develop strategies

To conclude, we shall briefly cover three techniques that can be used during the phase in which the most possible solutions are searched for: brainstorming, the Delphi technique and the nominal group technique.

Brainstorming

Brainstorming is a method of suggesting unprepared solutions to a problem that come to mind spontaneously. This method is especially distinguished by the freedom with which the people who are confronted with the problem seek solution strategies. As soon as the problem is clear to all participants, the group members are asked to react spontaneously. They may say anything that comes to mind, without asking themselves if it is crazy, foolish, stupid or unfeasible. Moreover, they are asked to allow themselves to be inspired by the statements of others, to associate with them, or to elaborate upon them. All orally expressed strategies are listed and written on a board or flipchart. There are a few guidelines for the brainstorm phase:

- criticism is not accepted
- encourage the production of many different ideas
- encourage associations and combinations.

Delphi technique

In the Delphi technique group members react on paper to each other's individual contributions. When the question is clear to everybody, all participants think up as many possible solutions and write them down. The individual contributions are copied and distributed to all participants. Each participant comments on the strategies of the others and perhaps hits upon new ideas. All comments and new ideas are again distributed to all participants, when they are once more commented on. This process is repeated until the group has come to an agreement about what is the best strategy.

Nominal group technique

The nominal group technique is a combination of both the preceding techniques. The participants do not speak with each other during the first phase of the meeting. They sit around a table, are informed about the question, and work individually on the solution strategies. One by one the participants suggest a strategy that they have thought up. This is repeated until there are no more strategies to be contributed. All strategies are written on a board or flipchart. The group comments on each solution strategy. Then each participant places all contributed solutions in order. The strategy that scores the highest is ultimately chosen.

Figure 12.1 presents an overview of how to go about decision making.

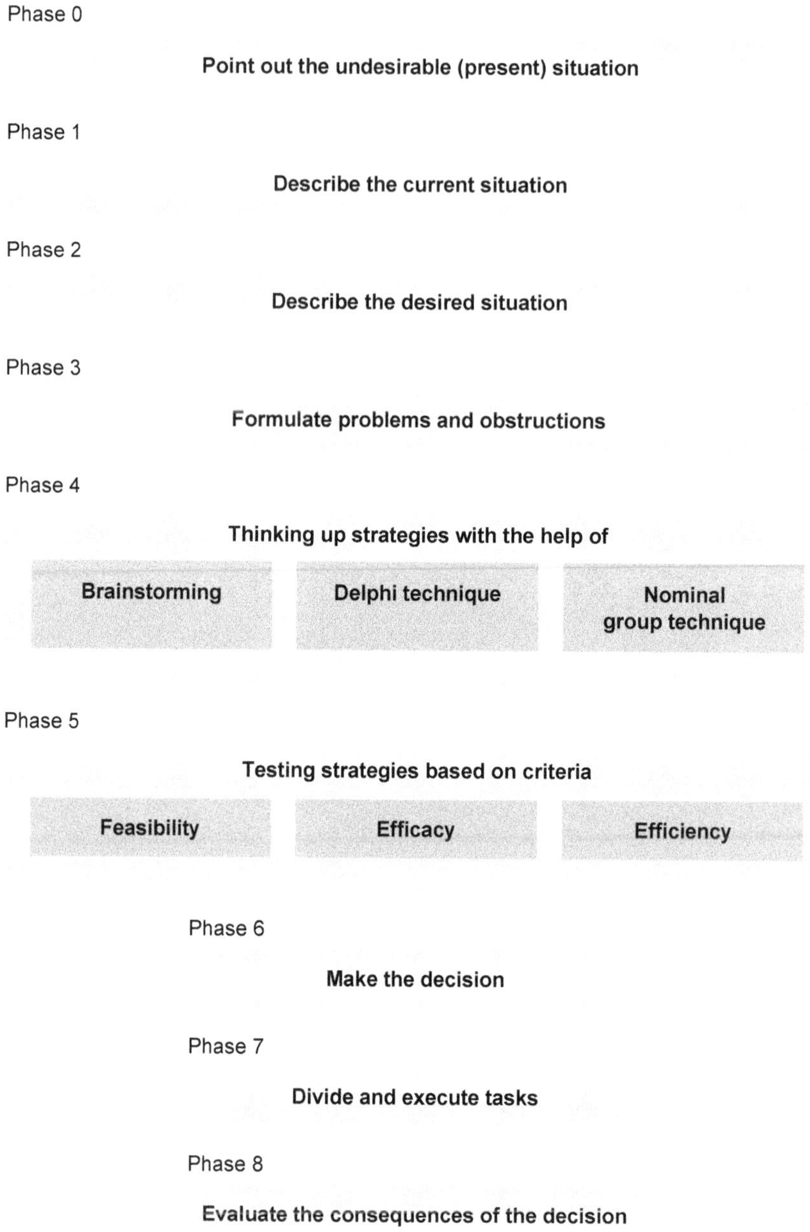

Phase 0

Point out the undesirable (present) situation

Phase 1

Describe the current situation

Phase 2

Describe the desired situation

Phase 3

Formulate problems and obstructions

Phase 4

Thinking up strategies with the help of

| **Brainstorming** | **Delphi technique** | **Nominal group technique** |

Phase 5

Testing strategies based on criteria

| **Feasibility** | **Efficacy** | **Efficiency** |

Phase 6

Make the decision

Phase 7

Divide and execute tasks

Phase 8

Evaluate the consequences of the decision

Figure 12.1 Overview of decision making

13 Leading meetings

Practical example

Over the last few years, absence due to illness has increased a fair amount at Dinner Ltd. Despite all the good intentions to increase employee participation in decision making, absence due to illness figures remain rather high. Managing Director Freddy Fortune attended a symposium on absenteeism control and was so inspired by this that he wants to bring the problem to the attention of his colleagues once again. He has acquired a few new ideas. First, he wants to explain the problem in a clear way. He then wishes to discuss with managers the possibility of determining a strategy that can reduce absence due to illness within a predetermined time period. He drops in on Charlotte Cohen and asks for data registered by administration about absence due to illness. They concentrate on the data to see if it is useful for them to have it recorded in neat graphs and tables. Charlotte knows her job. All the details can be processed within a few days, categorized into time periods, departments, age categories, sex, and level of education. Together with Freddy Fortune, Charlotte analyses the data. After that Freddy and Charlotte organize a meeting with the middle managers Bert Berman and Harry Haddock and the headwaiters Alex Armstrong, Grace Green and Ronald Rosenthal.

Introduction

A number of questions arise when discussing the theme 'leading meetings'. Why is the meeting being held? What is expected from participants in the meeting? Who has to do what? How should a meeting be held? In this chapter we discuss the *goals* of the meeting, the *various roles* that participants in a meeting fulfil, the difference between *task-oriented* and *people-oriented* behaviour, the *tasks* that must be performed before, during and after a meeting and the *structure* that best fits the goal of the meeting. At the end of the chapter we provide an overview.

Goal

It is very important that participants in a meeting realize in advance the goal of the meeting. This prevents a great deal of obscurity and expectations that cannot be realized. The meeting proceeds more efficiently if all participants pursue the same goal. For example, a meeting can be meant to inform the participants of new plans, to put a problem before them, to think up new strategies, to divide tasks, or regularly to go over the state of affairs. Depending on the goal of the meeting, a choice of structure must be made and possibly a choice regarding the direction of decision making.

In general, four different goals may be distinguished: formation of an opinion concerning a certain problem, making comments on a proposal, making decisions and allocating tasks in order to execute the decisions:

> The first goal of the meeting that Freddy and Charlotte have arranged for the managers of Dinner Ltd is to inform them about the figures of absence due to illness in the company, so that they can form a picture and an opinion. The second goal of this or maybe a subsequent meeting will be the development of strategies to reduce absence due to illness, and a decision to be made about the implementation of this.

Roles

At most meetings the following three roles can be classified: the chairperson, the minute taker and the participants.

Chairpersons should have the capacity to lead the meeting, to stand above the other parties, not to push their own opinion, to keep an eye on the structure, to cut short long-winded participants in such a way that they do not feel rejected, to stimulate participants and to guard the atmosphere as well as the time. In short, they must ensure that the meeting achieves its goal. This means that the problem is amply discussed, the information is given, the tasks are divided and the proposal is handled. At the same time, they must ensure a good relationship between all the parties. In other words, they must be equally task oriented and people oriented.

It is expected from *minute takers* that they can give an orderly and relevant summary of the discussion and different kinds of information that fly across the table. It is not expected that they make large contributions to the discussion. The minute taker is more an observer than a participant.

The *participants* have much more freedom in their behaviour than the chairperson or minute taker. Their specific task consists of talking and thinking together about the various points on the agenda, but the way in which they do so does not appear at first sight to be bound by any regulations. We would however like to plead that participants also become more aware of behaviour that contributes constructively to the smooth running of a meeting.

Task-oriented and people-oriented behaviour

The distinction between task-oriented and people-oriented behaviour applies to all those involved in a meeting. We now explain what we mean by these concepts.

Task-oriented behaviour is the result of an appropriate attitude in relation to the goal of the meeting. In order to demonstrate this attitude chairpersons should make use of the skills that we discussed in Part I. When listening, they should use the skills of attentive behaviour, asking open questions regarding the opinions of those present, asking closed questions for more factual information, concreteness to get a clear picture, and paraphrasing to show understanding participants' opinions. In the role of sender they should introduce the subject, ask attention for it and give a clear picture of their own vision.

If participants do not listen or talk with one another and interrupt each other they are not demonstrating task-oriented behaviour. Digressing from and lengthy elaboration on the subject are also behaviours that do not contribute to an efficient and goal-oriented meeting.

Participants who operate with a 'hidden agenda' have a negative influence on the progress of the meeting. By 'hidden agenda' we mean that people have goals in their own minds which are not on the distributed agenda, and which they bring up in an unclear way. This unclear way makes it difficult for the chairperson to recognize that a different topic of conversation is being introduced, which is why it is also difficult to postpone the topic to another meeting. Such participants sow the seeds of confusion through their obscurity.

People-oriented behaviour demonstrates that one is giving attention to the views, thoughts and feelings of the other participants in the meeting. Usually, different participants have different opinions. It is important for the smooth progress of the meeting that each individual's opinion is respected. Emotions often play a role during meetings: for example, when involvement in a subject is high or when there is a great deal at stake. Sometimes participants may feel alone during a meeting if none of the other participants agree with their standpoint. Disappointment, irritation, agitation, fear, aggression, affection, contentment and relief are examples of emotions that may influence the decision-taking process. In many cases it is effective to show understanding of these emotions either as chairperson, or as a participant in a meeting. By showing understanding you are respecting such emotions and enlarging the possibilities of a fruitful discussion. A meeting rarely proceeds purposefully if one or more of the participants is so emotional that they can no longer think clearly.

People-oriented behaviour can be demonstrated by using 'paraphrasing' and 'reflection of feelings', as described in Part I. The application of these skills enables the participants to feel understood and accepted. Moreover, the difference between the rational considerations and the emotions behind them becomes more transparent. Besides 'paraphrasing' and 'reflecting feelings', the listening skills of 'asking questions' and 'summarizing' are useful for letting the other participants know that their contributions are taken seriously. If meetings are held in an atmosphere that is viewed as disagreeable by some participants, it is useful to apply these skills to correct the atmosphere. In Part I this skill is described as 'situation clarification' (see p. 28). Here is a practical example from Dinner Ltd:

> The other participants in the meeting could wrongly interpret the enthusiasm of Freddy Fortune, based on his optimism acquired during the symposium, if none of them asks why he is so enthusiastic. The energy with which he forwards his plans can be interpreted as martinetery and viewed as meddling in internal questions concerning absence due to illness. If Freddy does not notice this irritation, there is only a slight chance that the rest of the meeting will accept his plans.

Tasks

The tasks of chairpersons, minute takers and participants can be divided into three sections: tasks before the meeting, during the meeting and after the meeting.

Before the meeting

Chairpersons should prepare themselves about the content of the meeting: 'What is it about, and how are we going to approach it.' They compile the agenda that shows the programme of the meeting. In this programme there are usually a number of regular points and a number of specific points, which we come back to later in the chapter. The order of the general points is important for their discussion. By setting the order of the different agenda points, the chairperson weighs their importance. It is best to place the most important point at the top of the agenda, the least important at the bottom. It may also be useful to handle the points that promote a good atmosphere first. Further, it may also be useful to estimate the time necessary for each point, so that the participants know what is expected of them and they can all work together using the time constructively.

In a formal meeting the participants receive the agenda together with the invitation and the items which must be gone through in advance at least 48 hours before the meeting. The invitation states where, when, why, about what, with whom and how long the meeting will be held.

Chairpersons should also prepare themselves about the participants. They can decide on a strategy if they know who will take part in the meeting and if they can anticipate their expected contributions.

Chairpersons also hold responsibility for the arrangement of tables and chairs in the meeting room. An important criterion is that all those present must be able to look at one another for the advancement of good communication. For most people it is difficult to remain listening and participating attentively for several hours. It is therefore advisable to make use of a flipchart or whiteboard on which, for example, the phases of the decision-making process are shown, and the proposals offered or solution strategies contributed are noted.

Minute takers prepare themselves for the meeting by finding out which data should be included in the notes, the structure of the discussion of the various themes, and what form the notes should take. This can best be done in consultation with the chairperson. By data we mean the names of those present and those absent, reasons for absence, date and place of the next meeting, the standard agenda for the next meeting and other similar points which are set out by mutual agreement and belong to the meeting culture of the group to which the minute taker belongs.

The *other participants* at the meeting prepare themselves by reading through all documents accompanying the distributed agenda. If one wants to be fully prepared then one has to acquire information in advance that can support one's own arguments: for example, by being up to date on concrete data. It can also be most useful if one tries to understand the opinions of other participants: on which arguments might they base their views or determine their standpoints?

During the meeting

Chairpersons open the meeting by welcoming those present, introducing new participants, excusing absentees and asking those present if they would like to adjust the agenda by adding points or changing the order. Often, there is a fixed time schedule for the meeting, so that all present are aware of it and will attempt to discuss the points within the time limit. The agenda points and the themes are handled according to the agreed structure.

When discussing a theme, chairpersons first indicate the goal of the discussion. They gather the information that all participants should know in order to discuss the theme in a constructive way. Finally, if necessary, they announce the structure by which the discussion can take place. Then the discussion starts. Now, it is the chairperson's task to maintain the agreed upon structure and doing so they should show both task-oriented and people-oriented behaviour.

Minute takers have the task of separating the main and sub-issues during the meeting and making relevant notes based so that they can write a report after the meeting. The report serves the purpose of providing clarity on the topics handled during the meeting and the decisions which have been made on them, both for those present and those absent.

During the meeting the task of the *participants* is actively to strive together to create a fruitful meeting: that is to say, they must adhere to the agreements made about time, order and structure. This also means that they listen actively to other participants, make use of the information contributed, and clearly articulate their own proposals, opinions, insights and views.

After the meeting

Chairpersons should go through the draft version of the minutes with the minute taker before these are sent to the participants. In some cases this can avoid problems, by choosing a formulation together which cannot lead to misunderstandings.

The *minute taker* writes the report of the meeting as quickly as possible and distributes it. This report should be prepared as soon as possible: first, because the meeting is fresh in everyone's minds; second, because the participants are reminded well in advance of the start of the next meeting about the tasks and assignments to be carried out by them.

The *participants* read through the minutes and make a note of points which ask for further clarification, proposals for adjustments of sections of the text, or other comments or criticisms. Above all, the participants fulfil their agreements and ensure that they can give a short report of this at the next meeting.

Structure

The structure of the meeting is represented in the agenda. The agenda has a number of points that are often handled in a fixed order and has changing topics. An example of a much used agenda format is as follows:

1   Opening.
2   Items received.
3   Announcements.
4   Report of the last meeting (minutes).
5   Different topics.
6   Any other business (AOB).
7   General questions.
8   Closing/new date.

1   The chairperson *opens* the meeting by welcoming all those present – introducing new people or asking everyone briefly to introduce themselves – and asks whether the agenda is agreed upon.
2   Letters, brochures and reports that have been received since the last meeting come under discussion. Usually, the chairperson has made a selection of those items which are to be laid out on the table and those that merit more attention. Depending on the content of these items, decisions can be taken immediately or discussion can be moved to the next meeting.

3   The announcements are usually made by the chairperson. They concern matters of importance to all the participants. Participants can also make announcements of questions that need only be laid on the table.

4   The minutes of the previous meeting are offered for approval to the meeting. This moment provides the occasion to make proposals for altering the formulation and making comments or asking questions about the agreements that have been made. It is usual during the first round of formal meetings to give the occasion for making comments concerning the text of the minutes and in the second round for comments in pursuance of the minutes.

5   The discussion of the different topics is dealt with more extensively below.

6   AOB questions are raised by those present during the meeting and comprise topics which cannot be handled under any of the other points.

7   The general questions are meant to give each participant the chance to mention points that have not yet been brought up.

8   The closing of the meeting serves to thank all those present for their contributions to determine a date, place and time for the next meeting, and to end the meeting.

Discussion of different topics

In Chapter 12 we gave an example of a phase model for handling the topic 'personnel day' during a meeting of the staff association committee of Dinner Ltd. This phase model gives a general structure for the discussion of different topics during a meeting. The topic can be a problem about which the meeting must form a picture or opinion. The topic can also be a proposal. Such a proposal must be introduced and commented on by others. It can concern a question about which a decision must be taken, or a task that must be divided up and allocated. The changing topics can all have changing goals: picture forming and opinion forming, receiving comments, decision making or task allocation.

In the first phase of the model, the question is contemplated from all angles. The situation is charted, as it were. What is wrong exactly, why is the situation no longer satisfactory, what do we want to achieve, what are the obstacles, what are the consequences? It is the intention that the participants at the meeting get a better insight into the problems of the topic. The answers to these questions indicate the structure of the discussion about the topic:

At Dinner Ltd the topic 'absence due to illness' should also be discussed from all angles at a meeting with the managers, so that a clear picture develops of absence due to illness within the organization, and the participants can form an opinion about the problem. Charlotte's tables are a good aid to this. A next stage, or possibly a next meeting, can be dedicated to thinking of, or commenting on, proposals for the improvement of the absentee registration or changes in the personnel policy.

The chairperson can further the smooth progress of a discussion by asking the presenter of a proposal for an explanation. This person gives a summary and the chairperson next suggests a procedure for discussion of the proposal. Then it is the turn of the participants. They can give their reactions. It is wise to introduce some limitations here too: for example, by first letting questions be put to the presenter and only in a subsequent stage allowing the proposal to be criticized. One can also think of other procedures, for example, first letting each participant react separately, and only starting the discussion after this.

Sometimes there is full support for the proposal, sometimes participants suggest amendments, and it may also happen that the proposal is completely rejected. The chairperson and the person who made the proposal should be capable of handling the comments in a constructive manner. The participants should also be capable of delivering comments in a constructive way (the necessary skills are 'giving criticism' and 'reacting to criticism', pp. 26–30).

Shortly before the next meeting Freddy Fortune sends a letter to the department heads that includes a number of recommendations for the decrease of absence due to illness. It is the intention that this will be discussed at the next meeting. The recommendations are:

- all absence due to illness must be registered per person per day
- sickness must be reported to the head of the department, not to reception as before
- after two days the department head has to enquire with the patient how it is going
- with sicknesses of a long duration, the head of department should regularly visit the sick employee
- with every non-physical cause, it should be investigated if the task or the working atmosphere has anything to do with the absence due to illness.

At the meeting Freddy suggests his proposals and the other participants comment on them and give suggestions or recommendations.

When a problem has become clear and the proposals on how to approach it have been discussed, a decision will have to be made as to whether or not the proposals will be received and the consequences thereof accepted. The participants at a decision-making meeting will have to know what exactly is being decided on and how the decision was arrived at. The proposed decision is once more clearly stated by the chairperson after the preceding discussion. The way in which the decision is made depends on the formal character of the meeting. In meetings where a formal regulation prevails, one should certainly stick to that, in view of the decision making and compulsory voting. At less formal meetings the decision making per situation can be discussed together:

> After the proposals of Freddy Fortune have been extensively discussed the meeting of Dinner Ltd decides as follows:
>
> • Interviews with the employees will be held to find out why absence due to illness is so high.
> • The heads of departments will consistently and systematically register personnel members reporting themselves sick.
> • The administration develops a system that processes the data quickly and adequately, so that problem areas become noticeable.
> • The heads of departments will receive training on 'absentee conversations'.

Finally, in many meetings, the tasks arising from the decisions will have to be allocated. Therefore it must be clear who will carry out the tasks, what exactly these tasks consist of, and what means are available for the person who has to execute the tasks.

Figure 13.1 presents an overview of how to lead meetings.

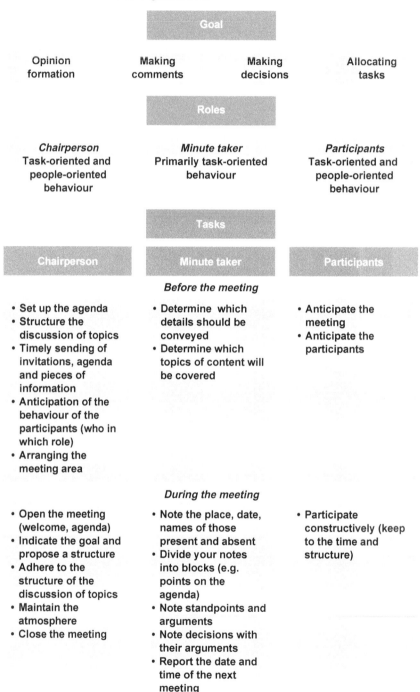

Goal			
Opinion formation	Making comments	Making decisions	Allocating tasks

Roles		
Chairperson Task-oriented and people-oriented behaviour	*Minute taker* Primarily task-oriented behaviour	*Participants* Task-oriented and people-oriented behaviour

Tasks		
Chairperson	**Minute taker**	**Participants**
	Before the meeting	
• Set up the agenda • Structure the discussion of topics • Timely sending of invitations, agenda and pieces of information • Anticipation of the behaviour of the participants (who in which role) • Arranging the meeting area	• Determine which details should be conveyed • Determine which topics of content will be covered	• Anticipate the meeting • Anticipate the participants
	During the meeting	
• Open the meeting (welcome, agenda) • Indicate the goal and propose a structure • Adhere to the structure of the discussion of topics • Maintain the atmosphere • Close the meeting	• Note the place, date, names of those present and absent • Divide your notes into blocks (e.g. points on the agenda) • Note standpoints and arguments • Note decisions with their arguments • Report the date and time of the next meeting	• Participate constructively (keep to the time and structure)

Figure 13.1 Overview of leading meetings

Tasks		
Chairperson	**Minute taker**	**Participants**
	After the meeting	
• Possibly go through the report with the minute taker	• Write the report as quickly as possible • The report consists of: — head with information — summary of the discussion with or without names – decision list	• Read the minutes and fulfil your agreements

Structure
Follow the agenda
Discussion of the topics

Discuss the problem/question

Describe the present situation	Describe the desired situation	Mention the problem and obstacles	Mention the consequences

Comment on proposals

Summarize the proposal	React to the proposal	Criticize the proposal	React to reactions and criticism

Taking a decision

According to the phase model in Chapter 12	According to regulations	According to incidental agreement

Allocating tasks

Agree who will do what, when	Motivate why it must be done	Agree to which standards the tasks must fulfil

14 Conflict management

Practical example

Commercial Director Gerald Glass and Managing Director Freddy Fortune have some problems about the costs of a new staircase for their building. It was built at the end of the nineteenth century and they intend to retain the classic style. They started the project a couple of months ago with the stair manufacturing factory Classic Stairs Ltd. The budget for the renewal of the old staircase threatens to be exceeded. If Gerald compares the financial review of this renovation with the amount originally agreed upon in the year's financial planning, it appears that the costs for the stairs are becoming too high. Freddy Fortune's opinion however is that the good ambience of a hotel is one of its most important features and that even though costs are higher than calculated in advance the improvements should go on. 'Costs precede benefits' is his motto. Freddy thinks that Gerald can be a bit narrow-minded sometimes. He is always precise about ensuring that not one penny extra is paid, as if he was paying out of his own pocket. Gerald on the other hand thinks that Freddy has too little regard for the economic aspects of Dinner Ltd and he doesn't seem to realize that the salaries have to be paid each month.

Introduction

We are talking about a *conflict* in a situation where people or groups (parties):

- have opposing ideas, views or opinions about a certain question
- view the situation as a conflict situation
- have emotions that play a part in the situation.

This chapter is first concerned with conflict between two people and how they can make use of certain skills to avoid or resolve conflict. The chapter then covers conflict between two people who are no longer in a position to resolve it without the intervention of a third party. We will discuss a number of characteristics of the conflict situation, conflict management behaviour, behaviour that evokes conflict, conflict management with the help of a mediator, and a conversational model that can be used either by two people who wish to resolve the conflict themselves, or by a mediator. We close the chapter with an overview.

Characteristics of conflict situations

Within a conflict situation the following characteristics can be observed:

1 *The point of difference*. The point of difference is the question about which the conflict is concerned. There are usually both rational and emotional aspects to a conflict:

> In the example of Gerald Glass and Freddy Fortune a rational question is whether or not the charge for the staircase is too high. The emotional aspect of their conflict is that Freddy considers Gerald to be narrow-minded concerning the ambience of the building, whereas Gerald views Freddy as having a tendency to waste money.

2 *Different interests*. In most conflict situations there are considerable differences in the interests of the conflicting persons or parties:

> In the example, the interest of Gerald Glass is to keep the company's financial affairs accurate. At the end of the year he is responsible for the balance between the costs and benefits of Dinner Ltd. Freddy Fortune's interest is that the company's building should have perfect style. He thinks that a good atmosphere will lead to a better image, and therefore in the end to more clients.

3 *Dependence*. In each conflict the degree of dependency of the conflicting persons or parties can be assessed:

> The mutual dependence is high in our example. Gerald and Freddy are together responsible for Dinner Ltd. In the future they still have to work together. So a good relationship between them is of great importance. It will give a bad impression to the other staff if they are 'fighting' with each other.

4 *Power*. In situations where the power of the parties is unequally distributed, the more powerful person can solve the problem by using this power. Sometimes this is necessary. However, the question is whether this strategy will lead to positive consequences. The less powerful

person has not been able to participate in the solution and will most likely resist the consequences:

> Freddy has the power to overrule Gerald's resistance. However, this might lead to a disturbed relationship.

5   *Time pressure.* This is an important element in the resolution of conflicts. If there is no time to go into a thorough discussion of the dispute, there is a great chance that a solution will be forced. The consequence is that one party or both feel compelled to put up with a solution with which they are unhappy. Therefore, the risk exists that the parties are not motivated to carry out the decisions. However, in some situations a shortage of time can lead to a compromise on a question that would otherwise have been prolonged:

> In the example of Freddy and Gerald, there is a shortage of time because the staircase must be installed before a certain deadline. This is probably a factor that helps them to reach an agreement about the costs.

Conflict management behaviour

Depending on personal characteristics and the specifics of the conflict situation, people 'choose' certain behaviours to resolve a conflict. Here, two general ways or styles of conflict management can be distinguished. Two personality characteristics are underlying these ways or styles:

- the tendency to accommodate the wishes of the other party
- the tendency to promote one's own interests.

Blake and Mouton (1977) argue that as a consequence of these general personality characteristics people may develop a preference for a certain behavioural style when they have to manage conflicts. The authors discuss five dominant conflict styles that people may have developed based on their personal preference:

1   Avoiding or running away from the conflict.
2   Adapting to the other and covering up the conflict.
3   Negotiating with the other in order to reach a compromise.
4   Fighting the other as an adversary, forcing them into a solution.
5   Working together to reach a solution.

Blake and Mouton (1977) illustrated these conflict handling styles in a diagram (see Figure 14.1). The X-axis shows the extent to which one is

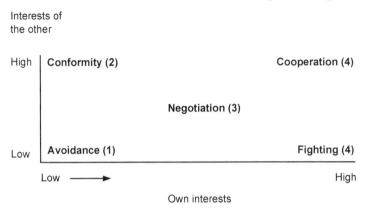

Figure 14.1 Conflict management styles

inclined toward promoting one's own interests. Analogously, the Y-axis shows the extent to which one is inclined to take the interests of the other into account. The five conflict management styles can be placed in the area bordered by the axes.

Description of the conflict management styles

We now describe the five conflict management styles. We should emphasise that these forms are extremes. In general, people use mixes of these extreme forms, depending on the situation in which the conflict has arisen. We first give a description of the form at its extreme and the type of people to whom this style matches in every situation. Then we describe situations where the *conscious* choice for that specific style can be effective.

Avoidance

When people have little tendency to promote their own interests and simultaneously do not attach much importance to the interests of others, we speak of conflict avoidance. People falling into this category tend to think there is nothing wrong with it. Maybe these people always avoid conflict because they are not ready to change something in their situation and are afraid of being turned down if they would try to do so.

Not getting involved in conflict can also be a *conscious* choice that may be sensible in specific situations: for example, in situations where people are convinced that they have no chance of winning or where they are too afraid of the other party; or in situations where they do not feel responsible for the question, do not find the question important enough, or do not think that the time has come to tackle the conflict.

Conformity

When one scores low on the dimension *own interests* and high on the dimension of *others' interests*, there will be a tendency to conformity. This second rather passive method of conflict management can be based on personality structure, characterized by a tendency to efface oneself and to be continually focused on others. Such people want to remain in favour, are afraid of rejection, and find it impolite to promote one's own interests. People who usually conform are often very dependent on the judgement of others and have little self-confidence.

However, there are situations in which people consciously decide to conform: for example, if they see that the question is of greater interest to the other party than to themselves. When people want to demonstrate their goodwill, in some situations they might conform so as to build up social credit in this way. For example, in one situation they may give in so that they can show less flexibility in another situation and the other party must then demonstrate their willingness. There are many situations in which it is important to maintain good relationships.

Negotiation

Negotiation is a style of conflict management where on the one hand both parties strive for their own interests, but on the other try to maintain a good relationship. So the score is in the middle on both dimensions (own interests and others' interests). Negotiation differs from cooperation (discussed below) in that one is trying to realize the best results for oneself, whereas in cooperation both parties are striving for the best result for each side. In some situations it is apparent in advance that a maximum result is impossible for both parties, and an acceptable solution is striven for: a compromise. Some people expend a lot of energy negotiating on every question in every situation, however trivial.

In resolving a conflict one can also *consciously* choose the negotiation strategy. The goal then is to strive for a compromise by making concessions on both sides. The choice of this strategy can be made if both parties are dependent on each other and the question is equally important to them both. Chapter 15 deals with this strategy extensively.

Fighting

Scoring high on the dimension of own interests and low on the dimension of the others' interests leads to a fighting conflict management style. By fighting we mean behaviour that is intended to win the conflict. People who always tend to fight are characterized by an all-or-nothing attitude towards the question, even at the expense of the other party.

A *conscious decision* to adopt a fighting style can be chosen in situations that are so important that one doesn't care about the desires and needs of the other party. Examples include:

- situations where one is convinced of the reasonableness of one's own standpoint and the unreasonableness of the standpoint of the other party
- situations where one is so emotionally involved that one is not prepared to make concessions because it concerns a question of principle in which one's own values and norms are at stake
- situations in which one is subject to time pressure so that it is impossible to enter into lengthy negotiations or to cooperate.

Cooperation

High scores on both dimensions lead to a conflict management style of cooperation. When parties cooperate they show behaviour that is intended to maximize the results for both sides. Both parties try to maintain a good relationship with the other and to attain a reasonable solution for the conflict. This situation is also known as a 'win-win' situation (Gatchalian, 1998). People who work together devote a great deal of time and energy on the maintenance of good mutual understanding and strive for satisfactory results for both parties. People who use this strategy usually have a lot of self-confidence, are not preoccupied with the self and can put energy into imagining the feelings and thoughts of the other party. They are usually creative in thinking up solutions that are attractive to both sides.

In order to cooperate it is necessary that both parties have the intention to work together. Cooperation is a strategy that demands many communication skills from both parties. A *conscious choice* of this strategy means that both parties want to maintain an optimal relationship with each other and are willing to invest time on this purpose.

We have now given an overview of a number of different conflict management styles. There are two passive styles – avoidance and conformity – and three active styles – negotiation, fighting and cooperation. Many people usually approach conflicts in the same way based on their personal style and often they are not conscious of what this style is. However, it is often more effective to make a conscious decision about one of these styles depending on the situation and question concerned. One then consciously chooses a strategy to manage the conflict adequately.

Behaviour that evokes conflict

In this chapter we have concentrated so far on individual styles of managing conflict. Apart from this personal style, people often show behaviour that may evoke or intensify a conflict. Sometimes people are unaware of this kind of behaviour. In general, behaviour that evokes or intensifies conflict is causing irritation in the other. Examples of such behaviour include:

- holding endless monologues
- interrupting the other
- presenting excessive arguments in support of one's own vision
- making unreasonable proposals
- using debating tricks ('Surely you yourself believe.' 'Mrs X, an expert in this area, believes')
- asking suggestive questions.

Conflicts can also arise because people feel themselves to be personally attacked:

> In our example of the conflict at Dinner Ltd, Gerald Glass would create conflict if he addressed Freddy Fortune in the following manner:
> 'Freddy, once again there is something totally wrong with your budget for the staircase. Take a look – £30,000 pounds for ten little stairs. Don't you think this is unbelievable!'
> Gerald's suggestive accusation and deprecating use of words ('once again', 'totally wrong', 'little stairs') cause Freddy to become irritated and react:
> 'Don't get on your high horse, Gerald. It really looks as if you're having to pay it out of your own pocket.'
> So, Freddy goes into a counterattack by accusing Gerald of being too penny-pinching. This conflict could swiftly escalate because the relationship between the debating persons and not the question under discussion become the topic of conversation.

In order to avoid or dilute conflicts, it is best that one remains clear about one's own intentions, stays receptive to the ideas of the other, and avoids behaviour that provokes irritation. Here are a number of suggestions for behaviour that may prevent the escalation of conflict:

1 Speak in I-terms ('I understand that . . .', 'I notice that . . .').
2 Speak for yourself ('Nevertheless, I view this differently').
3 Ask for the other's opinion ('What do you think about it?').
4 Direct the conversation to the question and not at the person ('It involves a lot of money' and not 'You're wasting a lot of money').
5 Do not enunciate certainties ('Of course we all know that').
6 Avoid the use of the words 'always' ('You always think only of your own interests') and 'never' ('You never think of the financial consequences').
7 Keep the doors open ('Should you wish to come back to this . . .').

8 Do not break off the negotiations ('I do not wish to come back to this again').

9 Make suggestions to reach a solution ('Shall we ask someone else for his opinion?').

Conflict management conversations

When two persons have different opinions concerning a certain question, they have to discuss this in a conversation. One of them will have to take the initiative and invite the other to try and reach a solution together. Careful *preparation* of such conversations may be helpful to clarify the question.

It is important that both parties are aware of the 'real problem'. There are often different layers that play a part at the same time. Sometimes disturbed relations (*relation conflicts*) underlie *business conflicts*: for example, a difference of opinion concerning tasks that have to be executed in an organization. Then a first goal should be to repair the confidence in the relationship between the parties. If that goal can be achieved, it will be easier for both parties to find a solution to the business conflict. Apart from the rational and emotional aspects of the question, both parties also have to prepare *how they want to make their points*. They should think of their own arguments and how to give criticism and how to respond to the arguments and criticism of the other party. It is often useful to make a list of your different points on paper. When you have these to hand, it is easier to pay attention to the views of the other party.

Both parties may create alternative solutions to the conflict during the preparation phase. It is advantageous to think of these solutions in a quiet atmosphere without being overwhelmed by the solutions of the other party. After this preparation phase the conversation may then be held following the four phases of the model described in the next section. The initiator of the conversation often takes the role of conversation leader.

Mediation: Conflict management with the help of a mediator

Some conflicts can only be resolved with the help of a third party. In general, a conflict that requires the help of an outsider will already have escalated. If the conflict has not yet escalated the parties can usually resolve it themselves. The third party may be requested or appointed by the conflicting parties to help resolve the conflict. The third party can also offer to help: for example, a head of personnel who notices that cooperation between staff members is not going smoothly because a conflict situation has arisen. We now discuss the role of the third party as mediator.

The aim of the mediator

When a third party mediates between two other parties, this mediator first has to discover what kind of conflict is involved. In general a conflict can be divided into its *content aspect* (the question concerned) and its *relational aspect* (the tense relationship between parties). Having analysed these aspects of the conflict, the mediator will strive for two goals. First, the mediator will try to reduce the tension between the parties. Only when this has been accomplished can the other goal be achieved: resolution of the question.

While some conflict situations are mainly concerned with rational questions, others may involve mainly emotional questions. If the point of difference is a rational question, the mediator can help resolve the conflict by, for example, making agreements or contracts or reaching agreement on a strategy or policy plan. With emotional questions the mediator can help by stimulating mutual understanding and acceptance of different opinions.

Skills of the mediator

First, a mediator must control the direction of the conversation using regulating skills (see Chapter 1). They should propose a structure for the conversation and try to maintain it. Furthermore, the mediator has to improve communication between both parties by making agreements on *how* the discussion will progress: for example, the agreement that both parties take turns to speak, allow one another to finish, and show that they are listening to each another by responding to what the other party says. Second, the mediator has to use listening skills (Chapter 2) such as asking questions and summarizing in order to clarify both parties' perspective on the question. By showing attentive behaviour to the conversation partners, asking questions, paraphrasing, reflecting feelings and making use of summaries, the mediator is the role model of an attentive listener. The mediator should also be creative in thinking of solutions that are acceptable to both parties. Finally, the mediator should stimulate the parties to find solutions themselves.

A model for conflict management

We now discuss a conversation model that is meant to resolve conflicts. We are assuming that a mediator is leading the conversation. However, this model can also be applied in a conversation between two or more people who wish to resolve a conflict themselves. It is not always possible to solve a question with a single conversation, sometimes more conversations are necessary. For example, when there has been a lot of escalation in the conflict, it is recommended to have separate interviews with both parties in order to form a first impression of the conflict situation. The conversation model for conflict management has four phases:

- opening phase
- exploration phase
- negotiation phase
- closing phase.

The opening phase

The mediator starts the opening phase by naming the reasons for the conversation. For example, the mediator has been asked to intervene by the conflicting parties. Possibly mediators have arranged the conversation themselves because they believe that the situation calls for it. The mediator emphasizes the danger of escalation if the conflict is not tackled and states that finding a solution together is in the interests of the organization and the parties concerned. Then the parties are asked to cooperate and try to reach a solution that is acceptable to both of them. There is absolutely no use in continuing the conversation if one of the parties is not prepared to cooperate.

The mediator firmly proposes the 'rules of the game' for the conversation: for example, allowing each other to finish, explaining views about the conflict in turn, not getting personal, and only talking about the question under discussion. In summary, the mediator makes use of his regulating skills by mentioning the reason and the aim of the conversation, by a specification of the time scale and by giving structure to the conversation.

The exploration phase

During the exploration phase the views of both parties are explored. The mediator first asks one of the parties to give their opinion of the question. At this stage the other party is not yet allowed to react. Then the other party may explain their standpoint. When both views have been voiced, the mediator gives a summary and checks whether both parties agree with it. After that both parties may react to one another. Parties should first ask questions for clarification and subsequently mention the points in the other party's story with which they disagree. At this stage understanding each other's viewpoints is promoted and an opening is created for constructive resolution of the conflict.

The mediator plays an important role in clarifying each party's opinions. By summarizing what has been said, by furthering accuracy and by asking for concreteness, the mediator can make sure that both parties have a clear picture of each other's opinions on the question. By asking the parties *to translate their complaint into a wish*, the mediator can further the development of willingness to reach a solution.

The negotiation phase

The negotiation phase is characterized by the making of agreements. After what has been discussed during the exploration phase, the mediator clearly summarizes the question once again. It is possible that the conflict consists of several elements that are easier to resolve one by one rather than the conflict as a whole. By first raising the earlier tabled issues which can be easily accommodated, the mediator puts the parties in a position to arrive at a solution. These small concessions bring the parties closer to one another step by step and smooth over the rough edges.

The mediator has the task of stimulating the parties to come up with solutions to the conflict and can be helpful by listing the pros and cons of the proposed solutions, thus creating a clear picture of the various alternatives. Mediators can also suggest solutions themselves if the parties are not in a position to do so.

The parties must be prepared to make concessions to their original starting position and thus attempt to come to a mutually acceptable situation. The mediator will do well to summarize the agreements and put them into writing so that no misunderstanding can arise about the promises of the parties.

Closing phase

The aim of the closing phase is to end the conversation in a succinct manner. Both parties now have a clearer picture of the perspective of the other party. The mediator announces the end of the conversation and possibly once again repeats the agreements. After that the mediator arranges that a copy of the agreements is made and makes an appointment for a subsequent meeting in which the agreements can be evaluated and possibly adjusted. Then the mediator investigates the satisfaction of both parties about the conflict and gives his opinion. With the help of this meta-communication, as yet unspoken resentments can still come to light and be worked out. Moreover, it promotes communication at future meeting(s). Figure 14.2 presents an overview of conflict management.

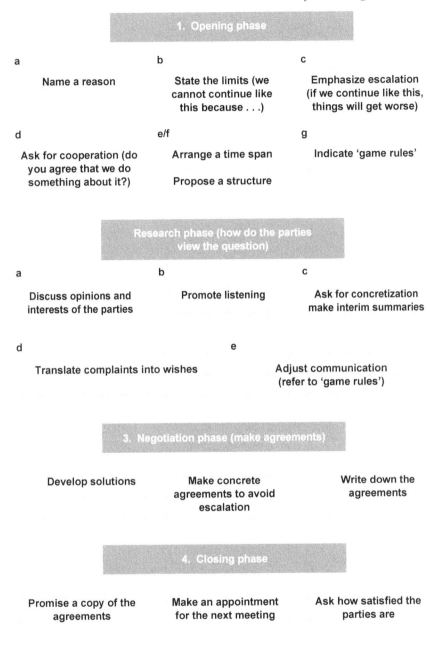

Figure 14.2 Overview of conflict management

15 Negotiating

Practical example

Not only does the staircase need replacing, but also 20 rooms on the third and fourth floors of Dinner Ltd need to be modernized. This involves the walls being repapered, windowframes repainted and new central heating on several floors. Commercial Director Gerald Glass has requested a quotation from the installation office of Central Heating for this last part. In the past Dinner Ltd has enjoyed good working relations with this company and has been satisfied with the jobs done. Gerald is to have a discussion with the installer about the price of the contract.

Apart from the cost of installation of new radiators, another point to be discussed is the schedule for the work, which is related to the price. If the installation of the radiators can be completed after the painters and decorators have finished, a great deal of work will be avoided. But then there is a very real chance of damage and the question is who will be responsible for paying for this. If the installation is completed before the painting company begins its work, then the radiators will have to be removed and again replaced. These are the points that Gerald Glass needs to negotiate with Central Heating.

Introduction

Negotiation is a skill that has been called a social achievement by Mastenbroek (1990). He means that people who have acquired this skill can make use of an instrument that allows them to influence many situations to their own satisfaction and to the satisfaction of the other party. In this chapter we discuss the negotiator's behaviour, the room for negotiations, different negotiation situations, negotiation skills and a model for the negotiation conversation. Finally we present an overview.

Negotiator's behaviour

Most typical of negotiating situations is the complexity of their goals and interests. On the one hand both parties have the same goal in mind:

reaching an agreement between themselves about the question. On the other hand each wants to achieve the most favourable results for themselves. The importance that the parties place on reaching an agreement is dependent upon the situation in which they find themselves and their position within that situation.

In Chapter 14 on conflict management, the skill of negotiating is described as behaviour directed at one's own interests and the interests of the other party. So it is clear that negotiation concerns not pushing your own interests at the cost of the relationship with the other party. The relationship should remain intact after the negotiations are complete. From this position – equally concerning oneself with one's own interests as with the interests of the other – the negotiator must continually choose between cooperation and fighting, and between conformity and avoidance. Negotiators should try to strengthen their own position, but should be cooperative in seeking solutions. In addition, they must try to obtain as much information as possible in order to find alternative solutions, as well as repressing the tendency to keep back too much information and rigidly retaining their own standpoint. If negotiators cannot represent themselves flexibly, the possibilities of reaching an agreement are limited.

In order to continue the relationship and simultaneously reach a favourable result, the game of bargaining – of giving and taking – must be played. This game requires space: the negotiation space.

Negotiation space

Negotiations are carried on in the existing space between the target points and the points of resistance of both parties (Carnevale & Pruitt, 1992; Whitney, 1990). The target point is the result that is viewed by one party as ideal. The point of resistance is the minimum result that one party wants to achieve. Figure 15.1 shows the target points and points of resistance of Dinner Ltd and Central Heating: It appears that in this situation the negotiation space is bordered by the amounts of £25,000 and £28,000. Dinner Ltd would preferably limit the expenditure to £23,000 and will strive for this during the negotiations. At most they are willing to spend £28,000. Central Heating wants to receive a minimum of £25,000 for the heating system, but strives for an amount of £30,000. Of course, neither party lets their points of resistance be known to the other. It is a case of cautiously putting out feelers to discover where the boundaries of the other party lie and what kinds of possibilities there are within the remaining space.

If there is no overlap between the negotiation spaces of either party, there is no room for negotiation. Then both parties will not be able to come to an agreement. In Figure 15.2 we present a situation that leaves no space for negotiation. It appears that Dinner Ltd is prepared to pay a maximum of £25,000 for the entire installation of the heating system. Central Heating does not want to install the system for less than £30,000.

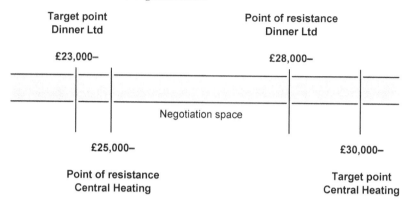

Figure 15.1 Target points and points of resistance: Negotiation space

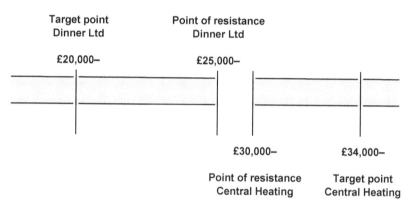

Figure 15.2 A situation without negotiation space

In practice people often negotiate about certain questions without formulating in advance a clear target point and point of resistance for themselves. In this case they are often caught out by the strategy of the other party and have nothing to contribute. The other party makes an offer, but wants to receive an answer in return.

Between target points and points of resistance lie the possibilities of coming to an agreement. By ensuring in advance that they have something to exchange, negotiators can enter the discussion well prepared. They then have the opportunity to make good use of the negotiation space.

The negotiation space is not only bordered by the target points and points of resistance. Psychological factors also determine this space. The importance that the negotiators attach to success in that particular situation, or the fear of loss of face, will reduce the room for negotiation. The desire to make a good impression on the opposing party can increase the negotiation space.

In an example from the negotiation situation of Dinner Ltd, imagine that rumours are going around that things are not going well with Central Heating since the departure of the previous company president. Then the company may consider it very important to attach its name to the renewal of Dinner Ltd's heating system. In such a situation the contractor of Central Heating could be prepared to be satisfied with less than the stated offer price.

Negotiation situations

The situations in which negotiations take place differ from one another as follows:

- the number of people who participate
- the subject
- the relationship between the negotiators.

Number of participants

As the number of participants in the negotiation increases, the situation becomes more complex and the tone more formal. In a dialogue the negotiators are directly concerned with one another. They decide upon the rules by which the communication proceeds. Negotiators with the best communication skills often have an advantage. They will usually also determine the tone of the negotiation and exercise influence on the process of affairs.

When more participants are involved in the negotiations, for example, three from both parties, usually a conversation leader or chairman is appointed to lead the negotiations according to an agreed upon procedure. The conversation often proceeds in a number of phases. Such a phase model gives support in bringing order to the complexity of the situation, allowing all the participants to have a chance fully to explore the negotiation space.

The subject

Negotiations are concerned with certain affairs. In many situations they are concerned with the distribution of money or goods. With this distribution the negotiation has a material question at stake. The distribution code must be negotiated: who receives what? In our example Dinner Ltd and Central Heating are concerned with such a distribution code.

In other situations the negotiations are about people: who is going to execute the plans that have been developed? How many hours do they need for that execution? Often in negotiations several aspects of personnel and payment are integrated. In our example Gerald Glass has to come to an agreement about the timing of the replacement of the central heating, on the number of persons who will execute the job, and finally on the costs of the project.

The relationship with the other negotiator(s)

Negotiators can differ from one another in many regards. The relationship can therefore be unequal. For example, the difference in age, function, experience and position can influence one of the parties favourably. For this reason it is advisable that negotiators who find themselves in a weaker position than the other party should prepare well for the negotiation situation. Even in a straightforward negotiation one can profit from preparing the conversation in advance.

Negotiating skills

There are four elements of the negotiation situation to be influenced by the negotiator:

- the negotiation space
- the positions
- the atmosphere
- the structure of the negotiation.

These elements cannot be viewed separately from one another. They influence each other: if changes occur in one element, they will have consequences for the other elements. For example, if the positions become harder, the atmosphere will deteriorate and the negotiation space diminishes. The influence of these elements demands from the negotiators adequate listening skills and the ability to provide clarity of their position.

Influencing the negotiation space

In order to influence the negotiation space, negotiators have to realize that behind most standpoints hides a motive. Why does the other party take this standpoint? What is the principle or idea behind it? What are the norms and values influencing the thinking and behaviour of the other party? What are your own norms and values? By asking questions, paraphrasing, giving reflections of feelings (see Adler, Rosen, & Silverstein, 1998) and summarizing, negotiators can discover the underlying interests. In addition, by providing insight into your own underlying interest to the other party, it can often appear that the negotiation contains more compatible interests than initially expected. Besides, it is easier to think of solutions if the negotiation space offers more possibilities than the black and white opposition of two standpoints.

Influencing positions

Negotiators are dependent on one another. They need each other in order to reach an agreement. However, this mutual dependence does not mean that they will both take an equal position.

> In the negotiations between Dinner Ltd and Central Heating, the installer would hold the best position if he were the only one in the geographical area. However, Dinner Ltd is in a luxurious position because there are more good installers. Shortage and time pressure can, amongst others, be factors that put one of the parties at an advantage and (temporarily) place them in the best position.

The extent to which negotiators can hold a good position depends on how much they are able to influence the situation. That is why it is important in a negotiation situation that negotiators realize in advance which positions they themselves and the other parties hold, and how these positions can be changed. By making a strength and weakness analysis of their own position and that of the other party, negotiators can get a good insight into the possibilities of influencing the negotiation. A way to strengthen one's own position is by thinking up an alternative in case the agreement is not made. With such an alternative up their sleeve negotiators are less dependent on the other party.

Influencing the atmosphere

One of the golden rules of negotiation (Piët, 1990) is to divide content and relationship. However firmly negotiators defend their affairs, they must ensure that they don't lose face. A negotiator who doesn't empathize with the person behind the other party creates an atmosphere of indifference. Good personal relationships contribute to negotiations proceeding in a relaxed atmosphere, wherein creativity regarding the solution can be developed. By expressing interest in personal affairs and by emphasizing the mutual dependence, an atmosphere can exist which is not solely 'businesslike'.

Influencing the structure of the negotiation

Effective negotiators will attempt, as far as possible, to influence the process of affairs during the negotiation. They can propose to allow the conversation to proceed according to a phase model (see Chapter 15). The addition of structure in the conversation leads to calmness in the negotiation situation. This usually has a positive effect on the atmosphere. The negotiation space can be extensively explored and the various alternatives get a chance to be considered and discussed. These activities demand a flexible attitude of negotiators. They have to be able to ask questions, to find alternatives and to think aloud about the proposals made by the other party. In short, they have to show explorative behaviour, directed to achieving an optimal result.

Model for a negotiation conversation

The negotiation conversation can be divided into five phases:

- preparation phase
- introduction phase
- exploration phase
- decision phase
- closing phase.

Preparation phase

We have already discussed how negotiators can influence four elements of the situation. Careful preparation is necessary in order to be able to do so. Negotiators should go through all the information about the question to be negotiated in advance. They have to set themselves goals and ask what the arguments are for different possible choices. Besides, it is useful to make an estimate of the goals of the other party. What do they want to achieve and why? At this stage the negotiators should think about their target point and point of resistance and the negotiation space in which they have to operate.

The preparation of positions takes place by making a strength and weakness analysis of both parties, by considering possible solutions and alternatives in case the negotiations do not proceed as desired. The atmosphere can also be anticipated in the preparation phase. For example, if the atmosphere is expected to be 'grim', then negotiators can plan to improve it by mentioning this grimness. Here, it is important to consider the difference between a stating and a supposing tone. A stating tone can influence the atmosphere negatively. If negotiators are aware of the personal background of the other party and show that this is relevant, this may improve the atmosphere. Finally, negotiators should prepare themselves on the structure of the conversation.

Introduction phase

Negotiators (or 'conversation leaders') who wish to negotiate in a structured manner begin the negotiation by indicating the goal of the meeting. They announce the time available and propose a procedure. The participants know what they can expect from each other and to what they must adhere.

Exploration phase

In the first round of the actual negotiation, conversation leaders recommend that the parties mention their wishes. They ask for the underlying interests and stimulate the participants to ask questions in order to clarify the situation. This phase is concerned with charting the starting points. It is the phase of asking questions and accepting: not of asking for justifications but for explanation. Negotiators often quickly feel threatened and unsure if they have to justify their wishes. Threatening leads to a defensive attitude. If there are no more questions for clarification, the conversation leader clearly summarizes the wishes and interests of the participating parties.

Discussion phase

After the conversation leader's summary the moment has been reached where the parties can begin to discuss each other's starting points and together seek common interests. At this phase the negotiation space is established. It is reinforced if small successes can be achieved at this stage that continue to play a role in subsequent proposals.

The conversation leader should take care that proposals are not immediately criticized and rejected, but are taken into consideration. Equally, the conversation leader should take care that proposals are not immediately embraced as the only solution. In this phase all proposals and solutions are viewed as alternatives (see p. 112; LePoole, 1991).

Decision phase

In this phase the parties suggest proposals for agreements and try to reach compromises. After all the explorations during the previous phases, it has usually become clear to the negotiators where the boundaries of the negotiation space lie. They now come forward with their proposals that will often, after a number of mutual concessions, lead to a definitive compromise. After one party's proposal the other can ask for time to think it over, for example, to find out for themselves how much elasticity remains in the proposal, or to deliberate with colleagues or with the group they are representing.

Closing phase

When the parties have closed their negotiations at the end of the decision phase, definitive agreements are made. It is often important that the agreements are laid down on paper. If necessary, the agreements are read aloud. The participating parties still have the opportunity of proposing a different formulation and can declare their agreement by signing the text. Then, no disagreement can come about concerning what exactly the agreement entailed. In order to reduce the danger of incorrect interpretations, it is important to formulate the agreements as clearly and concretely as possible. In some cases, even in simple negotiation situations, it is useful not to leave the agreements as oral, but to take note of the result and ask the participants to sign.

An overview of the negotiation process is shown in Figure 15.3.

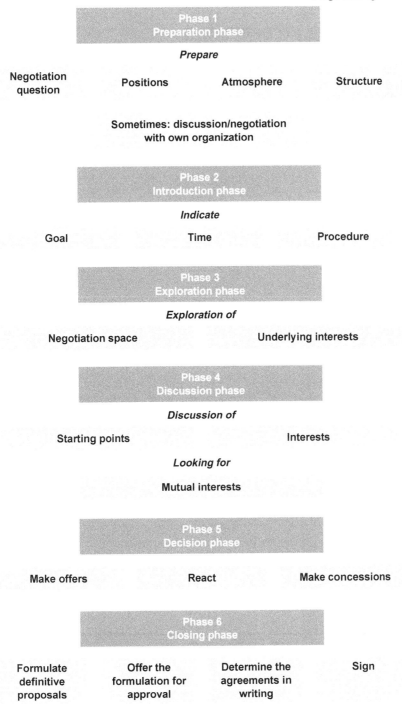

Figure 15.3 Overview of negotiation

16 Giving presentations

Practical example

Within Dinner Ltd there is an annual meeting in December concerning past achievements and future developments. Managing Director Freddy Fortune usually gives a presentation on these subjects. He writes his annual speech in cooperation with Gerald Glass. Although he is a good manager, Freddy has some difficulties in speaking in front of a large audience. He is always glad when he has fulfilled this part of his job. Now he has to prepare his speech. What exactly should his information be about? What should the staff know at the end of his presentation? Does he want to influence their attitudes in doing their work? Could he make use of the evaluations of the clientele about the service? What are the most important figures to be presented? Then, he should also consider the different educational levels of the personnel. When giving information on financial aspects, he should realize that many of them have only basic economic knowledge. It seems rather simple, this annual presentation, but now that it has actually come to it, first some questions must be answered before he can really make a start.

Introduction

In this chapter we will consecutively discuss the steps which a speaker has to make before during and after the presentation of a certain subject. Broadly outlined, the whole process of presentation can be divided into three phases:

- the preparation phase
- the presentation itself
- dealing with audience reaction.

During the preparation phase, the situation in which the presentation has to be held is analysed. The presenter considers a number of questions, looks for information and prepares his material. The presentation itself consists of three stages: the introduction, the core and the closing. One could say there is a 'head–body–tail division'. In the last phase the reactions of the audience must be responded to. In responding to the reactions, it is of primary importance that the person who asks questions or the one who has comments discerns that they are understood. The presenter must respond to the reactions as clearly as possible. At the end of this chapter the various presentation skills are summarized in an overview.

Preparation

In the practical example of Dinner Ltd we have already briefly touched upon a few questions that every presenter must consider in advance. First, they should ask themselves what they wish to achieve with the presentation. In short, what is the goal of it? Second, they should determine how they can achieve this goal. This is especially related to the structure of the presentation. Third, they should try to assemble sufficient information about the audience. Finally, they should gather information about limiting conditions. The investigation by Menzel and Carrell (1994) involving students showed that there was a positive relation between total preparation time and speech quality.

Goal

People can strive for different goals during a presentation. For example, the presenter wishes to convey information or desires *that the audience knows more about the subject* after the presentation than they did before. One can thus think of lectures, congresses or classes about a particular topic. It is also possible that the presenter wishes his audience *to adopt a different attitude* regarding the subject. One can thus consider a meeting in which the presenter wishes to support a certain controversial decision. In this case the aim is to convince the audience. In the third case, presenters can set the goal of *influencing the behaviour of their audience*. They want their audience *to do* something. Often these goals overlap. If presenters know how to convince an audience, they will develop a different attitude and usually adjust their behaviour.

> Freddy Fortune wants to convince the staff about the importance of friendliness to customers. He has too often heard complaints about this aspect, which is so important for their business.

Structure

During the preparation phase the presenter collects the information about the topic, prepares it and considers how to use it during the various phases of the presentation. The structure of a presentation consists of an introduction (head), a core (body) and a closing (tail). With the help of this division into three parts, the presenter brings order to the information. During the introduction, attention is captured and the audience gets an overview of the presentation. During the core phase the topic is handled, and during the closing phase the information is once again offered, in a compact way, and a final impression remains.

During the *introduction*, which takes up approximately 10 per cent of the time, the presenter should raise the interest of the audience. If attention is not first obtained, most of the presenter's efforts will be made in vain. The attention can be raised by, for example, first laying before the audience a small puzzle or rhetorical question. Some presenters are extremely ingenious in thinking up a short story, which can be told in a few sentences, or finding a proverb, saying or motto that relates to the content of the speech. Titles of popular books, television programmes or films are often sources of inspiration. Of course, it should apply here that the opening sentences are related to the rest of the presentation. Because it is difficult for the audience to understand what the subject of the presentation will be, it is useful to *give a clear overview* during the introduction of the order in which the subject will be handled and the time that is required. The audience then knows what to expect and when they can ask their questions.

The *middle section* consists of the core of the presentation and takes up about 80 per cent of the available time. The middle section is constructed according to the goal of the presentation. For example, if presenters wish to clarify a problem, they can list its causes and consequences and discuss them one by one. Should they wish to give a historical overview, then they could do this in chronological order. If presenters have to defend a standpoint, they can first list all the arguments that lead up to it, or they can first explain the standpoint and then mention the arguments that support it. Should presenters wish to ask for audience cooperation, they should first give an explanation of the necessity of the activities and then handle the process of affairs in a logical order.

During the preparation presenters structure their presentation and sometimes make a complete written version of it. However, reading out a written version often leads to audience boredom. To prevent this risk it is useful to note key words in the margin of the text that briefly summarize it. Giving the presentation using these key words allows presenters more opportunity to use common language. It looks as if they are speaking spontaneously, which is often more interesting for the audience. Should they suddenly lose the thread of the presentation, then they can always return to the written out text. It is self-evident that with this method presenters have to arrange their papers carefully to avoid nervous shuffling.

For the *closing* of the presentation, presenters need the last 10 per cent of the time. In this phase they should return to the question posed in the introduction. It is important that presenters come to solid conclusions, with a short repetition of the arguments already given. With the very last sentence the presenter can profit from the knowledge that people are equally alert, and remember a lot of information, at the end of the speech as they are at the beginning. Thus, the closing sentences can leave an ineradicable impression.

The audience

It is important that presenters realize in advance what the level of education of their audience is and have some knowledge of their colloquial language. Then they will be able to adapt their presentation to the (intellectual) level of the audience. People's abilities to abstract and generalize are dependent on their level of education and culture. The higher the level of education of the members of the audience, the easier presenters can make use of theoretical concepts. However, in most cases they would really have to make an effort to illustrate their presentation with *concrete examples*. Furthermore, presenters have to try to make an estimation of the prior knowledge of the audience in advance. If they are being confronted with the subject for the first time, then presenters will have to start by giving certain basic information. Finally, it can be useful for presenters if they are aware of the attitude that the audience adopts regarding the presentation of the subject and regarding the organization which they represent.

Limiting conditions

Before presenters start their preparation of the presentation, they should be aware of possible limiting conditions. By limiting conditions we mean the time remaining before the presentation must be given: the place where the presentation will take place, the possible aids necessary and the expected size of audience. Presenters have to ask themselves in advance what they can realize within these conditions. What work can they complete before the *date* of the presentation? It is recommended to estimate the time required for the preparation: collecting information about the target group, looking over accommodation, ordering and writing out materials, possibly making a PowerPoint presentation or overhead transparencies, watching slides, a video or film. All this often takes more time than one might imagine.

The *time* available for the presentation itself determines the amount of information that can be conveyed. A visit to the *location* where the presentation will be held in advance (if possible) gives presenters the opportunity to organize the optimal formation (chairs, tables, etc.) for the audience. Presenters must determine in advance what aids they need in order to achieve the goal of the presentation. Often a presentation becomes livelier through the use of PowerPoint, an overhead projector or audiovisual equipment. When presenting (yearly) figures such visual aids are vital. To demonstrate a conversation model in a skills training programme a videotape is useful.

However, the success of a presentation is not only dependent on the use of aids; sometimes too much use is made of them.

The expected *size of the audience* also influences the presenters' possibilities. Depending on the group size presenters will prepare a method of presentation. For example, they can only talk to a large group from a lectern and with the help of a sound system. With a small group they could possibly sit around a table. In a large group the opportunities to ask questions during the presentation are more limited than in a small group.

Giving the presentation

For many people it is difficult to process information that is only conveyed verbally. They are often quickly distracted, cannot concentrate for long periods at a time and remember selectively. In order to keep the attention and to make it easier for the audience to follow the thread, the presenter can make use of *expressive skills* (Mandel, 1987), *structure* and *text-supporting aids*.

Expressive skills

With the help of their expressive skills presenters can make use of their body and voice to support their words. Expressive skills can be divided into body language and use of the voice. Body language consists of the following skills: eye contact, facial expression, movement and posture (Argyle, 1988). Use of the voice consists of: speed of speech, timing, volume, rhythm of the sentences and articulation. We now give a brief description of these skills.

Body language

Using *eye contact* presenters get in touch with their audience and keep their attention. When they are alert to the responses of the audience, they can also try to accommodate their presentation.

With their *facial expression* presenters support and strengthen the emotions that fit their words. This may enhance the interest of the audience. *Gestures* also underline the meaning of the words, and hold the listeners' attention.

The *posture* of presenters expresses their state of mind. Posture can not only express enthusiasm, interest in the audience and self-confidence, but also disinterest, weariness, irritation or tension.

A natural use of these skills may have a positive influence on the effect of the presentation. An exaggerated or forced use of these skills will hamper the attention and is sometimes even ridiculous. To acquire and exercise these skills, presenters can simply practise at home in front of the mirror, or ask family or friends to comment on the effect of their body language.

Use of voice

A good *speed of speech* is one that is not so fast as to give a hurried impression or a nervous feeling, and not so slow as to decrease the attention or make the audience sleepy. With *timing* we mean the taking of breath and speech pauses at the correct moments. That moment can be a rest point for the speaker and the audience. A moment of silence can also be used to raise the attention for the sentence that is subsequently spoken.

Presenters have to adapt their *volume* to the acoustics, the room and the noise level. Besides this, *variation in the volume* more easily brings across the meaning that the speaker wishes the words to express.

The *intonation* is the melodic aspect of the speech. A good intonation supports the meaning of the words and holds the interest of the audience. A monotonous intonation is boring and causes frustration. A good *articulation* increases the comprehensibility and clarity as well as making it easier for the audience to keep their attention on the speech. Articulation means saying precisely and clearly all the syllables and sounds of a word.

In applying these skills presenters have to be aware that they can positively or negatively influence the successful conveyance of their presentation. An exaggerated use of these skills has the same effect on the audience, as does the exaggerated use of expressive body language, namely irritation, laughing or little attention to the content.

Maintaining the structure

The structure of the presentation can best be clearly indicated at the beginning in one of the first slides of the PowerPoint presentation, on a flipchart or transparency sheet. During their presentation presenters can refer to this structure. The advantage is that presenter and audience know where they are on the road to the end of the presentation.

Freddy Fortune gives the following structure to his annual speech:

1 Achievements in the last year.
2 Facts and figures.
3 Customer evaluations.
4 Future developments: The importance of customer friendliness.
5 Reactions.

For each point he has made subdivisions.

Another way to maintain audience concentration is by use of *linking sentences*. Every time a point has been fully discussed, presenters can ensure the audience keeps up by the use of a sentence with which they round off the previous point and introduce the next.

Freddy Fortune closes point 3, for example, with the sentences: 'Thus we see that our clients are not always fully satisfied with the different services. Some never come back for that reason. That is why I will now proceed to point 4: What do I mean with customer friendliness?'

Interim summaries can also be used to keep the presentation well organized and to hold the attention of the audience.

Text supporting visual aids

The use of a clear structure makes it easier for the audience to follow the presentation. Graphics and tables may also support the text. They can clarify the spoken text in the blink of an eye, but they should never be used in place of the text. Here too the audience must be taken by the hand, as it were, and led through the 'pictures' with the help of the presenter's words. As an example we remember the sick leave tables discussed in Chapter 13, which immediately clarified Freddy Fortune's words.

The use of whiteboard, PowerPoint, flipcharts and overhead projectors each has advantages and disadvantages. A major advantage of the use of a board is that the thought process of the presenter appears step by step on the board and the audience becomes involved in this. The audience sees the image growing. A disadvantage is that the text is often written quickly and thus sometimes carelessly. The advantage of a PowerPoint presentation is that it makes a professional impression. This modern technique also offers a lot of opportunities for a vivid presentation. The disadvantage is that rather often technical equipment stops working or doesn't work at all just at the beginning of the presentation. This can cause a lot of nerves in the presenter. There are two practical suggestions here. The first is to test the equipment before you give the presentation. The second is to have overhead transparencies just in case the technique fails. An advantage of the flipchart and overhead projector is that during the preparation the text can be written down on them. A disadvantage is that little or nothing can be added during the presentation. An advantage of the overhead projector over the flipchart is that typed text, especially large type, is clearly legible if you have used a large font.

Another possibility is to animate the spoken text with slides, videotapes or films. Often when using slides a great deal must be explained, whereas in contrast videotapes and films speak for themselves.

The major advantage of the use of these aids is that they are already available during the preparation phase and need only to be inserted at the right moment. In addition, they often give a lot of information in a short time, which remains better in the audience memory through the use of a combination of words and pictures. A description of the technical use of the different aids is beyond the scope of this text. If plugs need to be placed in sockets, one had better read the manual of the specific appliance rather than this book. We also omit here the practical use and many problems that can present themselves. The only comment we wish to make is that it is very irritating for the audience if the appliance does not work, or the user fiddles clumsily with the appliance. Also regarding this point, a solid preparation where the different aids have already been tested increases the chance of a successful presentation.

Dealing with reactions

When speakers have finished their presentation they may expect questions and comments. There are various ways in which they can stimulate the asking of questions and the making of comments and giving of criticism. The first way is by giving the audience the opportunity to ask questions if the presentation is not clear. The second way is by asking the audience to wait with their questions and comments until the presentation has been rounded off.

The advantage of the first way is that lack of clarity can be immediately solved. The audience thus remains very much involved in the story. But there are also a number of disadvantages related to this method. The audience often asks for further explanation that would have come up in the continuation of the speech anyway. Some listeners miss a little piece of information that will be repeated in a summary that still has to come. Members of the audience often think associatively. If they are informed of a situation they think of something similar and want to go into this. Different members again want to ride their hobbyhorses, and try to get attention on this via a question. Allowing questions to arise spontaneously can make the presentation very messy. The presenter loses the thread each time and the majority of the listeners are distracted from the direction of the speech. A solution for this is to ask the audience to react at once if there is a lack of clarity, but to hold their questions on the subject matter and comments for the discussion after the presentation. If one of the audience still makes comments on the subject matter during the speech, presenters can use the skill of 'situation clarification' (see p. 28). They could say, for example: 'I notice that you are posing a point to be discussed on the subject matter. Although I can imagine that it is interesting for you to get into this now, I would like to propose that you hold that point a moment, until I have finished my presentation. Do you agree with me?'

After their presentation presenters can expect various sorts of reactions. There are different kinds of questions. An interested listener may ask for some extra information; another might ask for the presenter's opinion; and there are questions from listeners who seem set on the goal of not letting a single opportunity pass without contributing their opinion. Sometimes questions are very clumsily and disjointedly expressed. Some people in the audience are determined to show their presence. In short, questions arise from totally different motives. But criticism may also come: criticism from listeners who do not agree with the content of the speech; who have a completely different vision of the question; who find the presenter has overlooked significant factors. In short, criticisms come from people who are not in agreement with the presenter, often for a multitude of reasons.

Presenters face the difficult task of satisfying all these people and improving the image of their organization through their way of reacting, or at the very least not negatively influencing it. Generally, there are two ways of reacting to questions. The first is by going into the question at once as clearly as possible, giving additional information on what is meant and observing if the person is satisfied with the answer. The second way is to briefly summarize the question. This method is especially useful if the question was not well understood or if the person first made an elaborate and complicated speech. Using this method the presenter gives the person the opportunity to ask the question differently or to adjust its formulation. Moreover, the summary gives presenters the opportunity to prepare their thoughts and time to formulate an answer.

When reacting to criticism, presenters can best confirm that other opinions are possible and emphasize the points they agree with. However, when they don't agree with the criticism, they may firmly say so. Here it is important that the person from the audience does not feel rejected and in order to save face strongly asserts his authority. A yes–no debate is usually not very fruitful and rapidly annoys the remaining listeners. The main point is that presenters deal with questions and criticisms respectfully.

Figure 16.1 illustrates how to give a successful presentation.

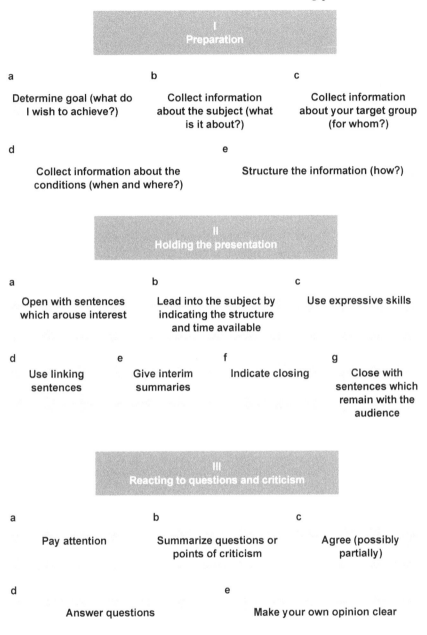

Figure 16.1 Overview of giving presentations

Appendix A
Exercises

Chapter 1   Regulating skills

1   Divide the total group into subgroups of three persons.
2   Within the subgroups divide the three people into three roles: the interviewer, the interviewee and the observer.
3   Hold the conversation.
4   Discuss the conversation afterwards according to the guidelines in Appendix B on role play.
5   Change roles and repeat the exercise. Make use of the learning points that have arisen during the previous exercise.

Exercise 1.1 Conversation about Part I of this book

Role of interviewer

You are going to have a conversation about Part I of this book. In this conversation first use the regulating skills mentioned in Chapter 1. These skills are now the focal point.

First, state in a short introduction what the purpose of this conversation is. Second, inform your partner about the duration of it. Third, inform your partner how you want to stage this conversation (structure and points of conversation should be indicated).

Prepare yourself for this conversation and try to keep to the structure that you have proposed.

Terminate the conversation when the time that you have indicated has passed.

For this exercise 5 minutes is sufficient.

Role of interviewee

You are going to have a conversation about Part I of this book. React just as you usually do.

Role of observer

See Appendix B on role play (pp. 186–191).

Chapter 2   Listening skills

1   Divide the total group into subgroups of three people.
2   Within the subgroups divide the three people into three roles: inter-viewer, interviewee and observer.
3   Hold the conversation (about 5 minutes).
4   Discuss the conversation afterwards, according to the guidelines in Appendix B on role play (pp. 186–191).
5   Change roles and repeat the exercise. Try to make use of the learning points that have arisen in the previous exercise.

Exercise 2.1 Attentive behaviour and asking questions

Role of interviewer

Try to find out what your partner's activities are apart from their studies. Make a choice to discuss one of these activities more extensively.

Role of interviewee

Imagine you are not very talkative. So, don't tell everything immediately. Answer with a yes or no if the interviewer asks closed questions. Only give more information when the interviewer is inviting and attentive.

Role of observer

See Appendix B on role play (pp. 186–191).

Exercise 2.2 Paraphrasing content and reflection of feelings

Role of interviewer

Try to get a clear picture of how your interviewee's previous semester has been going. Especially try to find out what the different activities were all about and in what kind of emotional situation your partner was during that period.

Role of interviewee

Try to answer the interviewer's questions frankly. Give special attention to paraphrases of content and reflections of feeling, and make corrections when these are wrong or not specific enough.

Role of observer

See Appendix B on role play (pp. 186–191).

Exercise 2.3　Concreteness and summarizing

Role of interviewer

Interview your partner about the jobs they have done apart from studying: for example, holiday work, part-time jobs, or occasional work in a student intermediary agency. Try to get a clear picture about the contents of these jobs, the experiences, the dealings with colleagues and superiors. At the end of the conversation summarize the work and ask your partner whether the summary was accurate.

Role of interviewee

Answer the interviewer's questions. Do not offer all the details about yourself, but give the interviewee a chance to get a good picture of all your working activities either before or after your studies.

Role of observer

See Appendix B on role play (pp. 186–191).

Chapter 3　Sender skills

1　Divide the group into subgroups of three people.
2　Within these subgroups divide the three people into three roles: interviewer, interviewee and observer.
3　Hold the conversation (5 minutes).
4　Evaluate the conversation, according to the guidelines in Appendix B on role play (pp. 186–191).

Exercise 3.1　Making requests and refusing

Let each person in the trio note down a request that can be made to one of the other persons. Then there are three rounds.

1　A makes the request to B in an assertive manner. B reacts in a sub-assertive manner. The observer (C) gives feedback on the behaviour of both A and B.
2　B makes the request in a sub-assertive manner. C reacts in an aggressive manner. The observer (A) gives feedback on the behaviour of both B and C.

3 C makes the request in an aggressive manner. A reacts in an assertive manner. The observer (B) gives feedback on the behaviour of both A and C.

Exercise 3.2 *Giving criticism and reacting to criticism*

Description of the situation

John and Peter are good friends. They live in the same house, both work, sometimes they go out together and sometimes they are by themselves. Lately the times they go out together have not been as much fun as they used to be. Peter drinks too much and keeps hanging on later and it occurs more and more often that John then goes home by himself. They have a silent agreement that what happened the night before is never discussed the next day.

Role of John

The relationship between you and Peter is not what it used to be lately. You believe he is drinking more and more. He eventually gets annoying and then starts to tell boring stories and plays practical jokes that are immensely stupid and sometimes very hurtful to others. He also has to be dragged away from these situations. If you say anything about this, he gets very angry and can be very unpleasant. You then decide to leave and go home. On the one hand you are annoyed because the evening was not much fun and on the other you are worried about Peter's condition. On top of everything else you feel embarrassed about his behaviour on nights like that. Although you are not used to discussing your nights out, you decide to do so now.

Role of Peter

Things have not been going well lately for you. The relationship between you and John has cooled off, although you two can still get along with each other. You go out together once in a while, but John seems unable to handle anything any more. He also often goes home early, saying that lots of things need to be done the next day, and then looks at you disapprovingly. You know that he thinks that you drink too much, but when John gets to act like a teacher, you just feel like staying on and going on for a while. Besides you really don't drink that much. You really know your boundaries.

Conduct this role play in three different ways:

1 John criticizes in the wrong way.
Peter reacts in the way he usually reacts in situations like this.

2   John criticizes in the right way.
     Peter reacts in the wrong way.
3   John criticizes in the right way.
     Peter reacts in the right way.

Role of observer

Evaluate each way separately. Pay especial attention to the effect that each of the different exercises has on the behaviour of both interviewees.

Exercise 3.3 Giving criticism and reacting to criticism

The goal of this exercise is to learn to distinguish assertive, sub-assertive and aggressive styles when using the skills of giving and receiving criticism. Time: about 30 minutes. Method: work in groups of 6 (A–F) and a trainer.

Step 1.   Each student writes down two points of criticism (for example, coming late, not keeping appointments).
Step 2.   The participants all get an action card and a reaction card. These cards have on them the following: sub-assertive, assertive and aggressive.
Step 3.   A gives B his points of criticism in the described manner (see card). B reacts in the described way (see card). C, D, E and F get the observation assignment: How does A give criticism and how does B react?
Step 4.   The trainer asks C, D, E and F what they thought of the criticism and makes their observations concrete by asking for specific behaviours they observed.
Step 5.   The trainer notes down the behaviour that characterizes sub-assertive, assertive and aggressive behaviour on the whiteboard. Mistakes can be made in encoding (for example, someone who acts aggressively while he means to act assertively) and in decoding (for example, someone who interprets sub-assertive behaviour as assertive).
Step 6.   Continue B→C.
             Round 1: 6 × criticism + 6 × reaction.
             Duration: approximately 6 × 2 minutes = 12 minutes.
Step 7.   Round 2: same.
             Assemble cards + hand them out again.
             Duration: approximately 12 minutes.
Step 8.   The trainer gives a summary according to notes on the whiteboard.

Chapter 4   Interviewing

Exercise 4.1 Interviews

Divide the group into two subgroups: group A and group B. First the members of group A interview the members of Group B. Then the members of Group B interview the members of group A.

Group A consists of a group of students who have to imagine that they are the staff of a student research company. The company has got the assignment to investigate the free time of students of higher vocational studies. The goal of this investigation is to be able to adjust and to use this 'need', maybe for a type of organized free time use for students. The association wants to get an insight into the time that students have apart from their studies, in which way they use it, and where the bottlenecks are regarding work load, travel time, housing, etc.

Group B also consists of students who have to imagine that they are staff members of a student research company. The company has given them the assignment to investigate the needs of students of local colleges for other types and forms of teaching methods. On the one hand they want maybe more individual tutoring, smaller exams and more feedback on reports and assignments. On the other hand they may need less personal approaches and lecturing and more written contact with the school through a personal computer connected to the computer network of the school, the teachers and the students. The following instructions hold for both group A and group B:

- Set up an interview scheme in small groups (two persons) for the investigation.
- Compare these schemes with each other's.
- Put together, based on this evaluation, with the whole subgroup a new interview scheme, which will probably be more extensive than the separate schemes.
- Put together, in groups of two, an interview plan (introduction, central part and closing) and divide the tasks for the staging of the interview. Who will do what and when?
- Stage the interview. Each pair of one group interviews a student of the other group. The fourth one (the second person of the other small group) is the observer.
- The observer evaluates the interview according to Figure 4.1 and the guidelines in Appendix B on role play (pp. 186–191).
- Discuss (in pairs) the information acquired during the interview in a report.
- Put together the evaluations of each subgroup into a report of either group A or B.

Chapter 5   The selection interview

See the exercise for Chapter 6.

Chapter 6   The job application interview

Exercise 6.1 Selection/job application

In this exercise both the skills of the selection interviewer and the skills of the job applicant are trained. For this exercise several sessions, preferably spread out over a couple of weeks, are needed. The exercise consists of three parts:

1   Preparation.
2   Writing and selection of application letters.
3   Selection/job application interviews.

1 Preparation

In the preparation stage each student chooses a personnel advertisement from a sample composed by the trainer. This advertisement is directed at the study profile of the particular group of students. Students have to argue their choice, making an analysis of the personnel advertisements. They should ask themselves the following questions: Is this job suitable for me? If so, why? Am I qualified for this job? If so, why? Moreover, students have to make an analysis of their strengths and weaknesses. In making this analysis they have to think of concrete examples of their strong and weak characteristics.

TASK

The students deliver their analyses of the advertisements and of their strengths and weaknesses to the trainer.

2 Writing and selection of application letters

The trainer starts with a selection of the personnel advertisements that gained the most interest. Then the group is divided into a number of subgroups; for each subgroup there is one personnel advertisement. Each member of the subgroup writes a job application letter and adds their CV. So each subgroup consists of members applying for the same job.

Each subgroup also represents the selection committee for another subgroup. So they also have to analyse a second personnel advertisement. Each subgroup assesses the application letters of another subgroup and comments on these letters.

TASKS

- Members of subgroup A have to write job application letters for organization B (subgroup B). Members of subgroup B have to write job application letters for organization C (subgroup C), etc.
- Members of subgroup B compose a list of criteria for the assessment of the job application letters of subgroup A. Members of subgroup C compose a list of criteria for the assessment of the job application letters of subgroup B, etc.
- Each subgroup assesses to what extent the content of the letters meets the criteria. The students in this subgroup also have to prepare a first rank order of the different candidates based on the scores on the criteria. They give their feedback in a plenary session. Each member of a subgroup gives feedback to a member of another subgroup.

3 Selection/job application interviews

PREPARATION

- Members of the selection committee prepare their selection interviews and have to make a scheme of subjects that have to be dealt with (see p. 43).
- They also divide roles: who will be the leader of the interview and who will be the members of the committee.
- Job applicants prepare their interview asking themselves the following questions: Which criteria of the job can I easily meet, which less or not? What are my strengths and weaknesses? How can I make clear that my capacities fit with the requirements of the job? How will I present myself?

TASK

Subgroups of selection committee members and job applicants deliver their preparations in writing to the trainer.

EXECUTION OF THE INTERVIEWS

The selection committee consists of a leader and two members. The other persons from the subgroup should act as observers. It should be decided which observers focus their attention to the skills of the selection committee and which observers focus on the behaviours of the applicants.

- The aim of the selection committee is to execute the selection interview according to the interview model (see Chapter 5) and to acquire concrete and relevant information from the applicants (see Chapter 5).

- The aim of the job applicants is to present themselves clearly and effectively. They should use the skills described in Chapter 6.
- The aim of the observers is to evaluate the selection/job application interview according to the guidelines of Appendix B on role play (pp. 186–191).

Chapter 7   The performance evaluation interview

Exercise 7.1 Performance evaluation interview

1   Divide the total group into subgroups of three people.
2   Within the subgroups divide the three people into three roles: interviewer, interviewee and observer.
3   Hold the interview (about 20 minutes).
4   Discuss the interview afterwards, according to the guidelines in Appendix B on role play (pp. 186–191).

Description of the situation

Dinner Ltd has hired a number of temporary waiters who might get a fixed appointment after one year when they fulfil the requirements of the job effectively. They have been informed that they will have a performance evaluation interview after six months.

Role of interviewer

You are playing the role of headwaiter (Alex Armstrong or Grace Green) within Dinner Ltd. You will have a performance evaluation interview with Stanley/Stephanie Stensen, who has now worked for six months within the organization. Think in advance of two points for giving positive feedback and two points of criticism. Then try to conduct the appraisal interview according to the conversation model in Chapter 7.

Role of interviewee

You are playing the role of temporary waiter Stanley/Stephanie Stensen within Dinner Ltd. You will have your first performance evaluation interview with headwaiter Alex Armstrong/Grace Green and you feel a bit nervous about that. Think in advance how you might feel to have fulfilled this job in the first half year of your appointment. Also think of one point of criticism you want to pass on to your headwaiter.

Role of observer

See Appendix B on role play (pp. 186–191).

Chapter 8   The personal problems interview

Exercise 8.1 'That difficult degree thesis!'

Description of the situation

It is not going well with student Reina. She has been studying for four years now and has met all the obligations of her course, except for her thesis. She has just returned from a training period abroad and has since lost all her motivation. Her student counsellor has only had a short talk with her over the phone in order to ask her whether she is considering graduating at the end of the year. In this phone call Reina confesses that she doesn't have the courage to fulfil her final obligations on a short-term basis. After a couple of weeks the student counsellor decides to contact her again in order to discuss the issue of graduation.

Divide the group into subgroups of three: the student counsellor/the student (Reina) and observer. Use the rules in Appendix B on role play (pp. 186–191).

Role of student counsellor

Although Reina has been a source of concern for you (she's been studying already for four years on a three-year course), you still find it very unsatis-factory if she quits now with the finish in sight. You do understand that the financial situation Reina is in does not look too good (her grant will be stopped) and you also know that written reports have previously been a stumbling block. The training period has also not been without troubles, but because the location was a company in Milan you have not been able to do much counselling. The training assignment was below the level of this education. Reina's remark that she has become less motivated regarding the remainder of her studies is a reason to invite her for an interview. You strongly suspect that there is more to it than the lack of financial aid. Besides, a solution could be found for that.

You are going to stage the interview according to the model in Chapter 8.

Role of Reina

You cannot see a way of graduating within a few months. In the first place you have the problem that your student grant will be cut. You must therefore find a way of getting the money. That already takes up much of your energy. Finding a job, working and studying all at the same time seems horrible to you at the moment. You shrink from the task of having to write your thesis. You have always found writing reports difficult and up till now you have made it so far because you have always worked in groups where you had to write a report together. Here you were always lucky that you had fellow students who could do the job. However, this final report has to be done by you and you actually don't have a clue what to write about, since in Milan you really did more bits and pieces of tasks than a whole task in itself. You really don't want to think about the final research project yet; you don't even have a clue about the subject.

Besides these study problems you also have another problem that has been bothering you very much lately. (Choose for this problem one that you are able to relate to easily, a situation that you have experienced or a situation that you know from a friend or acquaintance.) Touch on this subject too when you are having the talk with your student counsellor, when he or she turns the conversation in such a way that you feel comfortable discussing it. You do not feel that the student counsellor has anything to do with this or that he/she will be able to do something about it. It will depend on the situation whether you want to get into the subject or not. Do not act excessively closed and secretive so that the student counsellor does not get a chance to discuss it with you.

Role of observer

Evaluate this conversation according to the guidelines of Appendix B on role play. Take note: if there is no additional personal problem, the conversation can reach its objectives. The lack of motivation, the problems with writing reports, the financial limitations and the bad experience during the training period are Reina's personal problems.

If all participants prepare both the roles of student counsellor and Reina, roles can be switched within the group.

Chapter 9   Handling complaints

Exercise 9.1 Complaints

In this exercise first a list is made of students' personal situations where they had complaints to make (e.g. about a travel organization, a cold dish in a restaurant, etc.). Then these situations are role played in subgroups of three students.

Step 1. (total group) Students are asked to write down a personal situation where they had a complaint.
Step 2. The trainer makes a list of these situations on the whiteboard.
Step 3. The group is divided into subgroups of three students (A: complainer, B: person who has to deal with the complaint, C: observer).
Step 4. Each subgroup conducts three role plays. Those who have to deal with the complaint should use the conversation model and skills

discussed in Chapter 9 (see Figure 9.1). Observers should give feedback using the rules mentioned in Appendix B on role plays (pp. 186–191).

Chapter 10   Breaking bad news

Divide the group into subgroups of three. Each participant alternately plays the role of the breaker of bad news, receiver of bad news and observer.

Exercise 10.1 Bad news

Description of the situation

In their third year at a hotel management school the students have to write a (compulsory) report on an organizational theme. They do this in pairs. Quite a few hours of work are involved and the idea is that quite a lot of research is done and that it is written according to the specific guidelines for these types of reports. The teachers involved hold consultation sessions in order to keep an eye on the progress made with the reports. The students Bob and Anna are working together as a pair. They have already had two interviews about the progress of their report. The teachers were not very satisfied with what had been presented so far and are insisting that more time be put in on the report since the due date is in sight.

Role of Bob

You are working together with Anna on a report. Up till now you have invested more time on this than Anna since she still has some re-examinations and couldn't find the time. You have been to the library and conducted a literature study. You have also put the structure of the report on paper and have already written the introduction. You are not really getting much done, but Anna has promised to work hard on it from now on. You have decided to get together to discuss the progress of the report and to divide the work for the coming weeks.

Role of Anna

You are working together with Bob on a report. Bob has done all the work so far because you were busy with some re-examinations. You are really pushed for time. Apart from the exams there are also a couple of (private) matters (think of some) that will prevent you working on the report in the future. You decide not to hand in the report this year since you don't have time to work on it. Today you have a meeting with Bob about the progress of the report, but you are going to tell him that you won't be working on it any more and that you will put it off till next year.

Role of observer

See Appendix B on role play (pp. 186–191).

Exercise 10.2 More bad news

Description of the situation

In the undergraduate programme of a university twice a year a few hundred students go off on an internship. The 'internship office' therefore has two peak periods in which the secretaries, who work very accurately, are overloaded with work. Once in a while something goes wrong, but it is solved fairly quickly. Just before the training period starts the internship coordinators check whether everything is in order. Is the right student going to the correct location at the right time? They have a last information meeting with the students before they set off.

Role of student/trainee

You went to the last information meeting yesterday, just before you go off for your internship. You are going to do your internship in a company that deals in energy in another city. You are really excited about it. Everything is arranged and you have also been able to find a room. You have arranged that some friends will help you move in two weeks time. This morning the student counsellor called you to ask you to come to his office today since he wants to discuss something with you.

Role of student counsellor

Last night very late you were called by the internship coordinator. He has really bad flu and has not been on campus for a few weeks. The internship coordinator yesterday discovered a problematic administrative mistake. It seems that two students have registered for an internship with the same energy firm. However, the firm has specifically stated that it only wants one student. He has tried to arrange something else at the last minute, but without success. One of the two students has to be rejected, horrible as that is. It is the case that it has to be reported to one of the students as quickly as possible. Because the internship coordinator is ill, he has asked you to take care of this. In a while you will have an interview with one of the students whom you asked to come by this morning.

Role of observer

See Appendix B on role play (pp. 186–191).

Chapter 11   The sales interview

Exercise 11.1 Sales interviews

- Make a list within the group of personal items or services that fellow students would like to sell. Think about items such as PCs, video recorders, cameras, bikes, CD players, sporting goods, car pooling, summaries, software, etc.
- Make a list within the group of the interest there is for buying secondhand/used products or services.
- Arrange for sales interviews between the actual sellers and potential clients.
- Divide the group into subgroups of three: sellers, potential clients and observers.
- Stage the interviews according to the theory of Chapter 11.
- Observers should evaluate the interviews according to the guidelines of Appendix B on role play (pp. 186–191).

Exercise 11.2 More sales interviews

- Divide the group into two subgroups (A and B).
- Group A consists of students who have started their own little company that provides services to small companies (for example, the service of automation). Think about what kind of company it is, what type of service it offers and what could be done to make it interesting for potential clients specifically to buy this product or service.
- Group B consists of persons who either have their own companies or who are in a partnership. Think of a company yourself. Think of the type of product you might need, for example, certain automation programmes.
- Group A receives information about the goals of the company of Group B.
- Group A composes a plan about the product or service to be sold.
- Each participant in Group A visits one of the little companies in Group B and has an interview with the intent to sell.
- Observers should evaluate the interviews according to the guidelines of Appendix B on role play (pp. 186–191).

Chapter 12   Decision making

Exercise 12.1 Solving a problem

Choose with the entire group a problem for which you have to find a strategy to solve. For example:

- How do you improve the study behaviour of students of this school?
- How can you be a professional athlete and still graduate in four years?
- How can you find a room/house within 14 days?
- How can you get a lot of money within a month?

Divide the group into subgroups of four (A–D). Appoint a leader to each subgroup. Decide upon the time you want to spend (20 to 25 minutes will be enough).

Group A: Start brainstorming about the chosen subject.
Group B: Use the Delphi technique to come up with a strategy.
Group C: Use the nominal group technique in order to find a solution.
Group D: All participants think individually of as many strategies possible for the chosen problem.

When the arranged time has elapsed, compare the chosen strategies with each other in the entire group and discuss the techniques used. Make a list of the pros and cons of the different techniques.

Chapter 13 Leading meetings

Exercise 13.1 Organizing a conference

In this exercise there are four roles to be played: (a) leader of the meeting; (b) minutes taker; (c) participants at the meeting; (d) observers. For example in a group of 12 students there may be 7 participants and 3 observers. Depending on the time available the exercise may be repeated several times, so that more students play the role of leader of the meeting.

The subject of the meeting is the *organization of a conference* that is of importance to the students. The conference should be held during one afternoon or one day.

Role of leader of the meeting

Think in advance of a structure that you want to propose for the discussion. Then try to lead the meeting in accordance with the structure in Figure 13.1. The outcome of the discussion should be the time, place and programme of the conference.

Role of the minutes taker

Try to make minutes in accordance with the structure in Figure 13.1. Work out your notes after the meeting. Deliver your notes to the trainer.

Role of participants

Use your imagination to create a nice programme for the conference.

Role of observers

Observers should evaluate the meeting according to the guidelines in Appendix B on role play (pp. 186–191). Decide upon which of the observers will lead the feedback session.

Chapter 14   Conflict management

Exercise 14.1   Conflict management with the help of a mediator

Divide the total group into subgroups of four people. The exercise is a role play about conflict management with the help of a mediator. Three people are participating as student, teacher and mediator (head of department) respectively. The fourth person is the observer. To see differences in conflict management behaviour the exercise can be repeated after the first round.

Description of the situation

Teacher Simone Stewart has given student Louis Lowe a grade below pass level for his work on a practical on communication skills. If Stewart sticks to her decision Lowe will not fulfil the requirements for going on an internship. The consequence for Lowe will be that he will lose the next semester. Stewart supports her point of view by focusing on the minimal effort that Lowe has shown over the last semester. The interview report was all right, but the application letters and the other reports were barely passable. Lowe has never volunteered to participate in any role play. As an observer he didn't really do that well either. His observations were always vague. 'Oh, it was OK for me' was his general feedback. Besides that he was twice absent due to illness. To discuss this conflict Simone and Louis have agreed to invite Chris Clarke, the head of department.

Role of teacher Simone Stewart

Student Louis Lowe is the type of a student you cannot really figure out. He tries to get by with the minimum possible effort. During the training sessions he is hardly motivated. He always comes in moaning and groaning, prefers to keep his coat on during the entire class and looks around as if he really does not have a clue why he should be doing this. Sometimes he laughs along companionably. Besides the fact that his written work is barely passable, he has twice been absent. He said he was ill, but it's hard to believe that. Furthermore you have your doubts about whether he really participated in the interview project or whether his project partner did all the work. Because of all these reasons you have given him an unsatisfactory grade for his participation. However, Louis has not agreed with this. You have both decided to involve Chris Clarke, the head of department. You think that an example should be set with Louis and you are not about to make any concessions.

Role of student Louis Lowe

It really is not going too well with your studies. You can barely keep up with the pace. You still have lots of things to do in the evening, while many of your classmates are going out or have part-time jobs. You therefore view the training in communication skills as a waste of time. During that time you could be doing more important work for your other projects, which require a lot of studying. You have twice called in sick, because you could not get your work done any other way. However, you have done two make-up assignments instead that were not very much work. You have worked on the interview scheme with John (your partner for the interviewing project), but he did the interview by himself and has also written the report on it because you did not have time. You think that practising and getting feedback is really stupid. You had not expected that Stewart would flunk you because that seldom happens with practical training sessions. You are now in trouble because of the impending internship period. That failed grade needs to be changed into a pass! You have gone to Chris Clarke and he is willing to help the two of you to find a solution.

Role of head of department Chris Clarke

Student Louis Lowe has asked you to mediate in a conflict he has with one of the teachers of communications skills, Simone Stewart. Lowe has just not been able to convince her on his own. You have spoken with Simone Stewart on previous occasions but she was very determined in her opinion that this grade should remain a fail. When reviewing the case you still feel that a solution must be found: maybe an additional assignment in the area that the student clearly has not mastered yet. You know that Stewart suspects Lowe has not worked on the interview, but what can you do with suspicions. They have to come out into the open, otherwise this will drag on and on. You decide to hear the different views of the situation first.

Use the model on conflict management described in Chapter 14 (see Figure 14.1).

Role of observer

Observers should evaluate the role play according to the guidelines in Appendix B on role play (pp. 186–191).

Chapter 15   Negotiating

Exercise 15.1 The secondhand bike

Divide the group into subgroups of three: two negotiators and one observer.

Role of negotiator A

You are going for a cycling and canoeing holiday in France this summer. You have reserved two seats with your friend on the bus of the travel agency France Individuelle. The trip has been booked and paid for. However, this week your racing bicycle, which you bought last year, has been stolen. In view of the limited time you have till your holiday, you have to find a good secondhand racer really fast. You come across an ad in the local paper where a racing bicycle is offered for £300. It is two years old and has ten gears. You make an appointment to check out the bike.

Decide for yourself what you really want. What type of bike do you want for this holiday? What kind of extra things would you like it to have? Lights? Luggage rack? How much are you willing to spend? What is your best alternative if you can't find a usable secondhand bike within a week? Write all these details on a piece of paper. Negotiate with the seller of the bike. Try to use the overview from Figure 15.1.

Role of negotiator B

You have bought a couple of secondhand bikes. You have fixed up one of them and put it up for sale in the local newspaper at £300. The bike has ten gears and is probably two years old. You are planning to do the same with the other bikes but you really don't have the time right now since you still have to take some exams at the end of the semester. You are an enthusiastic racer and in order to make some extra money you buy and sell used bikes. You have a shed full of old but still usable bike parts. You want to buy yourself a new bike for £950 next month but you are £400 short.

Write down the minimum amount you want for the bike. Think before-hand what other possibilities you have to sell and replace spare parts. Also think of an alternative if the sale falls through. Also write these details on your piece of paper. Negotiate the sale. Try to use the overview from Figure 15.1.

Role of observer

Evaluate the way in which both negotiators have staged the meeting. Use Figure 15.1. Let the negotiators check which of the points they had written down were actually used. Evaluate the role play according to the guidelines in Appendix B on role play (pp. 186–191).

Exercise 15.2 Where to go on holiday

Divide the group into subgroups of three: two negotiators and one observer.

Description of the situation

A few months ago you arranged with a friend to go on holiday to Greece together. The friend is someone you usually get along with quite well, but not your best friend. It is holiday time now and if you still want to leave you have to book as soon as possible. Neither of you have any means of transport, nor any holiday equipment or cooking equipment. You have already tried borrowing or hiring it but you haven't succeeded, so it is easiest for both of you to book an all-in trip. The most luxurious trip costs £800 and the least luxurious costs £350. For £800 you get a deluxe hotel with sauna, swimming pool, tennis courts and a room with a bath, toilet, TV, stereo and telephone. For £350 you only get a simple room in a type of youth hotel without any facilities. Shower and toilet are located in the hall and you sleep in bunkbeds. Apart from these two options there are also other possibilities. For £550 you could have a good hotel with your own bathroom, but no other facilities. However, the hotel has a pool. For £650 you could have a fairly luxurious hotel. All bedrooms have bathrooms with bath, shower and toilet and there is also a television in the room. You both like a bit of luxury. For other expenses such as drinks, snacks and going out you have to calculate about £40 per day (you can make this as expensive as you like).

Role of negotiator A

You had arranged to save a good sum of money. That is why over the past three months you have worked practically every Saturday night as a waiter/ waitress in a pizzeria. You have also economized a great deal. You have saved about £900 and really want to spend it on a great holiday, preferably in a very luxurious hotel. Recently you bumped into another friend who told you that she too likes that sort of luxurious trip. Financially, it was no problem for her. She also told you that if your travel partner drops out she would like to go on holiday with you. She didn't feel like going with three people.

Today you and the friend with whom you made the original plan are getting together in order to decide how much money you want to spend on the holiday. First decide for yourself the amount of money you want to spend and then think of a negotiating strategy. Stick to the information that is provided.

Role of negotiator B

When you made the arrangement you were planning to save a lot of money for this trip and to find a part-time job. You did not manage to find the part-time job, but you have saved £750 through a lot of economizing. In the meantime you've found that you also want a new DVD player. You have just been offered a used one by a good friend of yours for £80. He is aware of your holiday plans and has already told you that you could pay him later for the DVD player, but in three months at the latest. You really don't want to take him up on this offer because you feel bad when you owe money, especially to friends.

Today you and your friend are getting together to decide how much money you want to spend on the trip. Decide for yourself first what the maximum is you might be willing to spend and also decide on a negotiation strategy. Stick to the information given.

Role of observer

Evaluate the way in which both negotiators have staged the meeting. Use Figure 15.1. Evaluate the role play according to the guidelines of Appendix B on role play (pp. 186–191).

Chapter 16   Giving presentations

Instructions

- For this exercise several sessions are required.
- Divide the group into presenters, audience and observers.
- Different members of the group prepare a presentation on a selected subject (for any suggestions see Exercises 16.1 and 16.2).
- Some of the others act like an audience.
- The observers make use of the observation forms below and then evaluate the presentation. In advance the learning points of each presenter are asked. (What do you want us to pay especial attention to?)

Exercise 16.1 *Making a presentation*

Choose in advance several members of the group to stage a presentation according to the rules described in Chapter 16. The goal can be, for example, fundraising for an association of which presenters are themselves members. Should any members of the audience want to contribute money to the association after the presentation, the presenter should be pleased. Think about things like Amnesty International, Nature Heritage, World Wild Life Fund, local foundations for the preserving of specific natural habitats or cultural environments, or the sponsoring of a local athlete. The goal of the presentation can also be to found a group within the school that will deal especially with the problems of the immediate environment.

Exercise 16.2 School presentation

Your high school is organizing a large party in celebration of its seventy-fifth anniversary. You were fairly active on the school student board and have now been asked to give a small presentation of 15 minutes, as an alumnus of the school, which should review previous years. Make use of any additional attributes. The audience consists of alumni, students, parents, teachers and former staff members and friends.

Observation form assessing expression skills

The observation form shown in Box A.1 lists the skills of the presenter that you have to assess. Mark as follows either during or after the presentation:

- if you find that the presenter is using the skill well = +
- if you feel that the presenter is not using the skill too badly, but could still improve = ±
- if you feel that the presenter uses the skill inadequately or not at all = −

Box A.1 Observation form assessing expression skills

	+	±	−
Eye contact			
Facial expression			
Gestures			
Posture			
Timing			
Speed of speech			
Volume			
Tone			
Articulation			
Fluency of speech			
Other			

Observation form assessing didactic skills

The goal of the observation form shown in Box A.2 is to observe whether and how the presenter uses the didactic skills during the presentation. The last two rows should include the presenter's learning points, which you should have to ask for in advance.

Box A.2 Observation form assessing didactic skills

	Remarks
Relating to the audience	
Structure	
Use of aids	
Contact with the public	
Learning point 1	
Learning point 2	

Appendix B
Role play

Because role play is frequently used on training programmes aimed at the acquisition of the skills described in this book, it is important to dedicate detailed attention to this kind of exercise.

Practising role play has the great advantage that it offers an opportunity to work in an atmosphere of freedom, meaning that mistakes and blunders are unimportant. You can freely experiment with new behaviour without having to be scared of hurting 'real' conversation partners. In a training session *prepared roles* are often used: first, because the majority of students do not have much experience with situations in a company setting; second, because the roles of conversation leader/interviewer and partner have to correspond. The duration of the conversations varies between 5 and 30 minutes. By using role play we can discern between:

- the preparation
- the preliminary talk
- acting and observing
- giving feedback.

The preparation

Good preparation is a minimum condition for the success of a role play. If you take the role of *conversation leader/interviewer* you must have a clear idea of the goal and structure of the conversation. You should also know which skills or conversation model you want to use and which of your weak points you wish to pay attention to.

If you take the role of *interviewee, applicant, client* or *employee (conversation partner)*, you have to imagine yourself in that particular role before the actual conversation.

For both parties it is equally valid that: when preparing a role, try to get a good understanding of the *environment and atmosphere* of the conversation. Try also to adapt your *attitude* and *use of language* as far as possible to the role. Students who are role playing a shop assistant will present themselves from a head of department in a conversation about the department's performance.

Besides prepared roles, *self-conceived roles* are sometimes used. Here also the following applies: play your role seriously. For example, choose a problem of somebody in your environment or something you yourself can well imagine. If you have to think about how old you are or whether you are married or not during the conversation both players can become somewhat confused. Last but not least, you should take into account the skills or conversation model practised by the conversation leader. Try to prepare the role in such a way that the conversation leader gets the opportunity to apply the skills or conversation model.

The *observer* should have a clear picture of the goal of the conversation, the structure and the relevant attitude and skills of the conversation leader.

The preliminary talk

The observer is the 'director' of a role play that is usually conducted in a trio. Before the role play starts, the observer goes over a number of points with the conversation leader. The conversation partner is not present here. The observer arranges with the conversation leader about how long the conversation will continue and who will keep an eye on the time (the observer or the conversation leader). As the observer you also discuss the conversation leader's learning objectives, so that you know what you should pay particular attention to. Also make agreements about what should happen if the conversation does not proceed smoothly. Does the conversation leader want to make it known that they want 'time out', or would they prefer that the observer intervene if necessary? In the eventuality of a 'time out' the conversation leader can discuss with the observer how the conversation could better be continued.

Acting and observing

It is important for the *conversation leader* to try and maintain their role. Of course, at any time when they are not able to continue they are allowed to have a break. However, before choosing this option we recommend that you try to find a solution yourself about difficult points in the conversation. This enlarges the learning effect.

If you play the role of the *conversation partner*, try to act your role realistically. Try to imagine how it would actually be if you really wanted a job and had to 'sell' yourself at a job application interview, or what it would be like to talk to your manager about a personal problem, or to receive criticism from your boss on your performance. It is very important to give the conversation leader the chance to practise their role. So, neither try to make it extremely easy nor extra difficult for the conversation leader.

The *observers* should not disturb the role play. Their task is to register the communication between conversation leader and conversation partner and to note down which skills the conversation leader has actually practised. By means of their observations and feedback, the observer helps the conversation leader to sharpen their communication skills. The conversation leaders thus receive a good picture of how they performed during a conversation and how this performance influenced the process of the conversation. On the basis of these observations, they can try to change their behaviour in subsequent conversations. To reach this goal – behavioural change – the observations must be given in concrete terms. Vague observations about how the role play went in general give the conversation leader little clarity. In such a case they don't learn how to change their attitude and behaviour. To observe everything which happens during a conversation is really an impossible task. So you have to make choices. In order to give useful feedback as observer you should always have the following points at the back of your mind:

- What is the goal of the conversation?
- What skills does it concern?
- What is the function of the skills in question? It is on this point that you must be able to give a comment after the conversation.

The information you wish to have after the conversation is:

- What did the conversation leader do and say during the conversation? Which skills did they use? What is your comment on the application of the skills?
- Were the skills used in a functional manner? What was their effect?
- How did the conversation partner react?

Giving feedback

Immediately after the role play the *conversation leader* first gets the opportunity to 'let off steam'. What is their opinion bearing in mind the goal they had set themselves? How did they feel? What were the difficult moments of the conversation?

Second, the *conversation partner* can give their impressions: What did they think of the attitude and behaviour of the conversation leader? How did they feel about it? What would they have liked to be different?

Third, the *observer* gives their impression of the conversation briefly and with concrete headlines. Has the goal of the conversation been achieved? Was the structure adhered to? What is their opinion on the attitude of the conversation leader?

Finally, the observer should offer systematic feedback with the use of notes made during the conversation. This feedback focuses on the *(basic) communication skills or conversation model to be practised* and the possible *learning points* of the conversation leader.

It is important for both parties to realize that this feedback is based mainly on the behaviour of the conversation leader during this conversation in interaction with the behaviour of the conversation partner, and not on their (total) personalities.

It often happens that a conversation does not proceed as planned. Certainly it is difficult for a novice conversation leader to keep an eye on everything. So, a lot can go wrong! This is not a problem at all and is often very instructive. However, in practice it appears that many trainees find it difficult to pass criticism to their fellow trainees. 'Did I see it right?' 'Isn't that unkind?' 'Later it will be my turn and maybe it's not so important.' Although these questions are understandable, constructive feedback is necessary to a good learning process. The following considerations may facilitate the observer:

- It concerns giving feedback on certain communication skills, conversation models, or learning points. Businesslike criticism is restricted to this and does not involve any negative comments on the character of the conversation leader.
- By accompanying your criticism with, for example, a question – 'What did you hope to achieve with your (re)action?' – and by contributing your own alternative or a better (re)action, the discussion becomes more concrete.

If the observer has finished giving their feedback according to the guidelines mentioned above, and if one of the trainers is present as an extra observer to the role play, then they get the last word: first, to give any additions to the observer's comments; second, to give feedback to the observer on the way in which they registered the role play and their observations and feedback.

It may be clear that not only a lot is expected from the conversation leader and conversation partner, but also from the observer. At the beginning of a training programme it will definitely not be simple to fulfil all the requirements of an observer. Sometimes you are not able to determine which skill the conversation leader applied or what the effect was of a certain intervention. It is helpful to develop an observation system for yourself, in which you can quickly note your observations and recount them during the evaluation. An example of such a system is shown below. To help you *record* a role play we have created a *short guide*. Box B.1 illustrates an example of a method of observing.

Box B.1 Observation system

Conversation leader's learning points:		
Conversation leader	Conversation partner	Observer
Note utterances in keywords	Note utterances in key words	• Mention the skills
. . . .	. . . .	• How do you evaluate this (e.g. +, –)?
. . . .	. . . .	• Alternatives, suggestions (. . . .)
. . . .	. . . .	• General impression of (e.g.) conversation style atmosphere, conversation leader's posture, eye contact, etc.
. . . .	. . . .	
. . . .	. . . .	
. . . .	. . . .	
. . . .	. . . .	
. . . .	. . . .	
. . . .	. . . .	
. . . .	. . . .	

Short guide for the observer

Besides observing, it is the task of the observer to watch the time and to allow the preliminary talk and evaluation of the role play to proceed as efficiently as possible. This overview is very useful during training sessions.

Preliminary talk

1   Discuss with the conversation leader:
   • the specific skills or the conversation model
   • learning points.
2   Make agreement on:
   • duration of the role play and evaluation
   • time out and intervention of the observer.

Feedback

1   Give the conversation leader the opportunity to 'let off steam'.
2   Ask the conversation partner to give their first impressions.
3   Give *short* feedback yourself on:
   • achieving the goal
   • adhering to the structure
   • attitude of the conversation leader.
4   Give both the opportunity *briefly* to react on this.
5   The observer gets the opportunity to structure their observations.

6   For each phase:
    - indicate which skills were used functionally
    - which skills were not use functionally
    - give suggestions for improvement
    - give the conversation leader (and possibility conversation partner) the opportunity to react.
7   Offer a summary in terms of 'old' and 'new' learning points.
8   Offer the trainer (if available) the opportunity to give extra feedback on the conversation leader's skills and on the observations.

References

Adler, R., Rosen, B., & Silverstein, E. (1998). Emotions in negotiation: How to manage fear and anger. *Negotiation Journal, 14*, 161–179.

Alberti, R., & Emmons, M. (2001). *Your perfect right: Assertiveness and equality in your life and relationships* (8th ed.). Atascadero, CA: Impact.

Argyle, M. (1981). *Social skills and work*. London: Methuen.

Argyle, M. (1988). *Bodily communication* (2nd ed.). New York: Methuen.

Argyle, M. (1995). Social skills. In N. Mackintosh & A. Colman (Eds), *Learning and social skills*. London: Longman.

Argyle, M., & Cook, M. (1976). *Gaze and mutual gaze*. Cambridge: Cambridge University Press.

Axtell, R. (1991). *Gestures: The do's and taboos of body language around the world*. New York: Wiley.

Baron, R., & Markman, G. (2000). Beyond social capital: How social skills can enhance entrepreneurs' success. *Academy of Management Executive, 14*, 106–116.

Benjamin, A. (1987). *The helping interview with case illustrations*. Boston: Houghton Mifflin.

Blake, R.R., & Mouton, J.S. (1977). *Leiderschapspatronen [Leadership patterns]*. Utrecht: Het Spectrum.

Bostrom, R. (1990). *Listening behavior: Measurement and applications*. New York: Guilford Press.

Brammer, L., & MacDonald, G. (1999). *The helping relationship* (7th ed.). Boston: Allyn & Bacon.

Burley-Allen, M. (1995). *Listening: The forgotten skill*. New York: Wiley.

Carnevale, P., & Pruitt, D. (1992). Negotiation and mediation. *Annual Review of Psychology, 43*, 531–582.

Chaplin, W., Phillips, J., Brown, J., Clanton, N., & Stein, J. (2000). Handshaking, gender, personality, and first impressions. *Journal of Personality and Social Psychology, 79*, 110–117.

Dickson, D. (1997). Reflecting. In O. Hargie (Ed.), *The handbook of communication skills*. London: Routledge.

Dickson, D., Hargie, O., & Morrow, N. (1997). *Communication skills training for health professionals* (2nd ed.). London: Chapman and Hall.

Dohrenwend, B. (1965). Some effects of open and closed questions on respondents' answers. *Human Organization, 24*, 175–184.

Egan, G. (2002). *The Skilled Helper* (7th ed.). Pacific Grove: Brooks/Cole.

Fowler, F.J., & Mangione, T.W. (1990). *Standardised survey interviewing: Minimising interviewer-related error.* Newbury Park, CA: Sage.

Gatchalian, J. (1998). Principled negotiation – a key to successful collective bargaining. *Management Decision, 36,* 222–225.

Gramsbergen-Hoogland, Y.H., & Van der Molen, H.T. (2003). *Gesprekken in Organisaties [Conversations in Organizations]* (3rd ed.). Groningen: Wolters-Noordhoff.

Greenspoon, J. (1955). The reinforcing effect of two spoken sounds on the frequency of two responses. *American Journal of Psychology, 68,* 409–416.

Hackney, H., & Cormier, L.S. (1979). *Counseling strategies and objectives.* Englewood Cliffs, NJ: Prentice Hall.

Hargie, O., & Dickson, D. (2004). *Skilled interpersonal communication* (4th ed.). London: Routledge.

Hargie, O., Dickson, D., & Tourish, D. (2004). *Communication skills for effective management.* Basingstoke: Macmillan.

Ivey, A.E. (1971). *Microcounseling. Innovations in interviewing training.* Springfield: Charles C. Thomas.

Ivey, A.E., & Bradford Ivey, M. (2003). *Intentional interviewing and counseling. Facilitating client development in a multicultural society.* Pacific Grove: Brooks/Cole.

Keats, D. (2000). *Interviewing: A practical guide for students and professionals.* Buckingham: Open University Press.

Korsch, B.M., & Negrete, V.F. (1972). Doctor–patient communication. *Scientific American, 227,* 66–74.

Korswagen, C.J.J. (1987). Het verkoopgesprek [The selling interview]. In J. Kolhuis Tanke, C. Korswagen, St. Verrept, & D. Depreeuw (Eds.), *Handboek Taalhantering. Praktische communicatiegids voor bedrijf, instelling en overheid [Handbook of linguistic usage. Practical communication guide for business, institution and government].* Deventer: Van Loghum Slaterus.

Kouwer, B.J. (1973). *Existentiële psychologie. Grondslagen van het psychologische gesprek [Existential psychology. Fundamentals of the psychological discourse].* Meppel: Boom.

Lang, G., & Van der Molen, H.T. (2003). *Psychologische gespreksvoering. Een basis voor hulpverlening [Psychological communication. A base for helping]* (11th ed.). Soest: Nelissen.

Lang, G., Van der Molen, H.T., Trower, P., & Look, R. (1990). *Personal conversations. Roles and skills for counsellors.* London: Routledge.

LePoole, S. (1991). *Never take no for an answer: A guide to successful negotiating.* London: Kogan Page.

Lewin, K. (1958). Group decision and social change. In E. Maccoby, T. Newcomb, & E. Hartley (Eds.), *Readings in social psychology* (pp. 197–211). New York: Holt, Rinehart, & Winston.

Mandel, S. (1987). *Effective presentation skills: A practical guide for better speaking.* Los Altos, CA: Crisp.

Mastenbroek, W.F.G. (1990). *Onderhandelen [Negotiating].* Utrecht: Het Spectrum.

Menzel, K., & Carrell, L. (1994). The relationship between preparation and performance in public speaking. *Communication Education, 43,* 17–26.

Millar, R., & Gallagher, M. (1997). The selection interview. In O. Hargie (Ed.), *The handbook of communication skills* (2nd ed.). London: Routledge.

Millar, R., & Gallagher, M. (2000). The interview approach. In O. Hargie, & D. Tourish (Eds.), *Handbook of communication audits for organisations*. London: Routledge.

Paterson, R. (2000). *The assertiveness workbook: How to express your ideas and stand up for yourself at work and in relationships*. Oakland: New Harbinger.

Piët, S. (1990). *Overleg, vergaderen en onderhandelen [Deliberations, meetings and negotiations]*. Groningen: Wolters-Noordhoff.

Roe, R.A., & Daniels, M.J.M. (1984). *Personeelsbeoordeling. Achtergronden en toepassing [Personnel assessment. Backgrounds and application]*. Assen: Van Gorcum.

Rogers, C.R. (1962). The interpersonal relationship: The core of guidance. *Harvard Educational Review, 32*, 416–429.

Russell, J., & Fernandez-Dols, J. (1997). What does a facial expression mean? In J. Russell, & J. Fernandez-Dols (Eds.), *The psychology of facial expression*. Cambridge: Cambridge University Press.

Steil, L. (1991). Listening training: The key to success in today's organizations. In D. Borisoff, & M. Purdy (Eds.), *Listening in everyday life*. Maryland: University of America Press.

Van der Molen, H.T. (1984). *Aan Verlegenheid valt iets te doen. Een cursus in plaats van therapie [How to deal with shyness. A course instead of therapy]*. Deventer: Van Loghum Slaterus.

Van der Molen, H.T., Hommes, M.A., Smit, G.N., & Lang, G. (1995). Two decades of cumulative microtraining in the Netherlands: An overview. *Educational Research and Evaluation. An International Journal on Theory and Practice, 1*, 347–378.

Veen, P. (1991). *Mensen in organisaties [People in organizations]*. Houten: Bohn Stafleu Van Loghum.

Voorendonk, R.H. (1986). Het slecht-nieuws-gesprek [Breaking bad news]. In J. Kolkhuis Tanke, C. Korswagen, St. Verrept, & D. Depreeuw (Eds.), *Handboek Taalhantering. Praktische communicatiegids voor bedrijf, instelling en overheid [Handbook of linguistic usage. Practical communication guide for business, institution and government]*. Deventer: Van Loghum Slaterus.

Vrolijk, A. (1991). *Gesprekstechniek [Communication technique]*. Houten: Bohn Stafleu Van Loghum.

Vroom, V.H., & Yetton, P.W. (1973). *Leadership and decision-making*. Pittsburgh: University of Pittsburgh Press.

Whetzel, D., & McDaniel, M. (1999). The employment interview. In A. Memon, & R. Bull (Eds.), *Handbook of the psychology of interviewing*. Chichester: Wiley.

Whitney, G. (1990). Before you negotiate: Get your act together. In I. Asherman, & S. Asherman (Eds.), *The negotiating sourcebook*. Amherst, MA: Human Resource Development Press.

Author index

Subject index